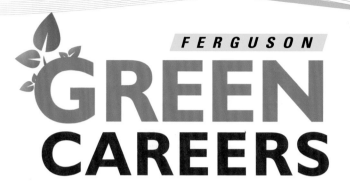

FERGUSON
GREEN
CAREERS

COMMUNICATION,
EDUCATION & TRAVEL

FERGUSON

GREEN
CAREERS

COMMUNICATION, EDUCATION & TRAVEL

PAMELA FEHL

Ferguson Publishing
An imprint of Infobase Publishing

Green Careers: Communication, Education, and Travel

Ferguson
An imprint of Infobase Publishing
132 West 31st Street
New York NY 10001

Library of Congress Cataloging-in-Publication Data
Fehl, Pamela.
    Communication, education, and travel / Pamela Fehl.
        p. cm. — (Green careers)
    Includes bibliographical references and index.
    ISBN-13: 978-0-8160-8154-7 (hardcover : alk. paper)
    ISBN-10: 0-8160-8154-9 (hardcover : alk. paper) 1. Environmental sciences—
Vocational guidance—Juvenile literature. 2. Green movement—Vocational
guidance—Juvenile literature. 3. Communication—Vocational guidance—
Juvenile literature. 4. Education—Vocational guidance—Juvenile literature.
5. Ecotourism—Vocational guidance—Juvenile literature. I. Title.
    GE60.F44 2010
    333.72023—dc22   2009048203

Ferguson books are available at special discounts when purchased in bulk
quantities for businesses, associations, institutions, or sales promotions.
Please call our Special Sales Department in New York at (212) 967-8800 or
(800) 322-8755.

You can find Ferguson on the World Wide Web at http://www.fergpubco.com

Text design by Annie O'Donnell
Composition by EJB Publishing Services
Cover printed by Bang Printing, Brainerd, MN
Book printed and bound by Bang Printing, Brainerd, MN
Date printed: April 2010
Printed in the United States of America

10 9 8 7 6 5 4 3 2 1

This book is printed on acid-free paper.

All links and Web addresses were checked and verified to be correct at the time
of publication. Because of the dynamic nature of the Web, some addresses and
links may have changed since publication and may no longer be valid.

Contents

Introduction   vii

Directors, Green Nonprofit Organizations   1

Directors of Volunteers, Green Nonprofit
Organizations   14

Ecomanagers, Green Hotels/Resorts   21

Ecotourism Agents/Planners   30

Environmental Activists   38

Environmental Education Program Directors   46

Environmental Educators   56

Fund-raisers, Green Nonprofit Organizations   67

Grant Writers, Green Nonprofit Organizations   75

Green Reporters   84

Inbound Tour Guides   92

Nature Photographers   102

Publicists, Green Nonprofit Organizations   112

Science Writers   121

Transportation Planners   130

Further Reading   138

Index   142

Introduction

Early environmentalists realized the importance of educating people about issues in order to motivate them into action. Naturalist John Muir triggered results in the 1800s through letter-writing campaigns to key legislators and policy makers in Congress. In the 20th century Ansel Adams used his nature photographs of certain regions in the United States to increase conservation efforts. People armed with knowledge are better prepared to take the steps needed to change the course of events. In his book, *The Age of Missing Information*, author, educator, and environmentalist Bill McKibben wrote, "What actually makes people happy is full engagement. You are most alive when working at the limit of your abilities." Engaging the general public is particularly crucial to environmental causes. Helping people understand the effects certain environmental issues have on health and quality of life and rallying for change is a task that professionals in the green communications, education, and travel sector take on with great enthusiasm and determination.

Volunteerism and activism are infectious—one person's passion for a cause often spreads and inspires others to follow suit. As Kathryn Cervino, Director of New York-based Coastal Preservation Network, states, "We found that many, many people love this town and are eager to volunteer and help their local environment. They simply didn't know how to get started, and just needed someone to take the lead." Environmental educators, activists, writers, photographers— all become interested in nature and the environment for any number of reasons. A book, news item, or conversation may set the spark. Or the passion can stem from a childhood whale-watching trip, or early years spent exploring the great outdoors. Specific inspirations for professionals in this field vary, but what all share is the desire to communicate what they learn along the way. All are taking the lead in keeping people up to date on local and global environment-related topics to stimulate dialogue and encourage critical thinking and informed decision making.

The jobs featured in this volume are a mere tip-of-the-iceberg sampling of the many different types of opportunities available in the green communications, education, and travel sectors. Included here are directors, green nonprofit organizations; directors of volunteers, green nonprofit organizations; ecomanagers, green hotels/resorts; ecotourism agents/planners; environmental activists; environmental education program directors; environmental educators;

fund-raisers, green nonprofit organizations; grant writers, green non-profit organizations; green reporters; inbound tour guides; nature photographers; publicists, green nonprofit organizations; science writers; and transportation planners.

Each job profile is divided into 12 sections to help you learn more about different aspects of the job, and to allow you to determine if your background, interests, and skills match the requirements.

- **Quick Facts** is a snapshot of job basics, including salary range and employment outlook.
- **Overview** summarizes in a few sentences the overall job responsibilities.
- **History** gives you background on the industry and job, highlighting issues and events in the past that influenced the profession, and pointing out founders and innovators in the field.
- **The Job** elaborates on daily responsibilities and what it takes to do the job well. Some profiles also feature comments and insights from people working in the profession.
- **Requirements** walks you through the educational requirements, from high school onward. **Other Requirements** describes the special skills and character traits that are an added plus in the work.
- **Exploring** offers suggestions for ways you can learn more about the job and industry. Here you will find recommendations for reading materials, professional associations, and other resources.
- **Employers** gives you an idea of industry sectors and types of companies that hire the featured professional. This section often includes statistics about the number of professionals employed in the United States, and top paying states and/or cities. Data is derived from the U.S. Department of Labor (DoL), the Bureau of Labor Statistics, the National Association of Colleges and Employers, and professional industry-related associations.
- **Starting Out** offers suggestions for steps you can take to get entry-level jobs in the field—whether through internships, building connections, or expanding knowledge and skills.
- **Advancement** shows the ways in which communications, education, and travel professionals can advance in the field.

✻ **Earnings** provides you with salary ranges for the job, based on data from the Bureau of Labor Statistics and other sources such as Salary.com and Payscale.com. Some jobs are relatively new and salary information is not readily available—in these instances, information is derived from nonprofit professional organizations or from employment organizations such as Idealist.org and SimplyHired.com.

✻ The **Work Environment** section describes the typical surroundings and conditions of employment. Also discussed are typical hours worked, any seasonal fluctuations, and the stresses and strains of the job.

✻ **Outlook** is a look into the future of the career based on current trends. Predictions are usually derived from DoL surveys, professional associations' studies, and/or experts' insights on the field.

✻ **For More Information** ends each profile with further resources you can use to explore the job, such as listings and contact information of professional associations you may want to join.

Directors, Green Nonprofit Organizations

School Subjects
Business
Communications
English

Personal Skills
Analytical
Creative
Decisive

Work Environment
Primarily indoors
Primarily one location

Minimum Education Level
Bachelor's degree

Salary Range
$27,770 to $68,680 to
$166,400+

Certification or Licensing
Voluntary

Outlook
About as fast as the
average

OVERVIEW

Directors of green nonprofit organizations manage nonprofit organizations that are focused on environmental issues such as cleaner air, lands, and waters; protection of wildlife species, habitats, and ecosystems; sustainable operations and policies; renewable energy sources and energy conservation; environmental laws and regulations; and a myriad of other green topics. They work closely with boards of directors and committees, manage staff, and oversee financial management of the organization. They are involved in all aspects of the organization, including fund-raising, grant writing, membership outreach and maintenance, programming and events, advocacy, marketing and promotion, and liaising with the media.

HISTORY

Nonprofit organizations are associations or corporations that conduct business for the benefit of the general public, without shareholders and without a profit motive. They may also be known as not-for-profit organizations. Although nonprofits do not operate for profit, they still file business documents and income statements, like for-profit businesses do, as mandated by federal, state, and local laws. Salaries for nonprofit employees are not considered expenses but rather necessities to run the organizations. The government monitors nonprofits closely to ensure that employees' salaries, expenses, and activities are in keeping with the organization's mission and budget. Excessive salaries and expenses that seem unrelated to the business usually trigger closer governmental scrutiny. If an organization is found to be misappropriating funds, the nonprofit status can be removed.

Nonprofits are organized to address a specific need within a community, region, or globally. Nonprofits may be focused on advocacy, arts, civic, cultural, education, or health and human services. All it takes is someone, or a group of people, identifying a need and deciding to organize a nonprofit group to help address this need. They can be organized and operated exclusively for scientific, charitable, religious, public safety, literary and educational purposes, for preventing cruelty or abuse to children or women, protecting animals, or fostering international sports and other cross-cultural programs. If the work they conduct is dedicated exclusively to the general public, nonprofits can be exempt from income taxes, or given tax breaks, depending on state regulations.

There are about 27 different types of nonprofit organizations under the Internal Revenue's Section 501 that meet the legal definitions for tax-exempt status. These can include churches, soup kitchens, charities, hospitals, colleges and universities, environmental groups, agricultural and horticultural organizations, labor groups, small insurance companies, public interest law firms, credit unions, film companies, television stations, theater companies, musicians' groups, museums, and the list goes on. The nonprofit sector is expanding every year. According to the U.S. Department of Labor, there are more than 1.64 million nonprofit institutions in the United States.

THE JOB

Directors of green nonprofit organizations are responsible for managing and overseeing all aspects of the business. They may have wide-ranging responsibilities and play larger roles (and work longer days) if the organization is small, or have fewer, yet more specific

Kathryn Tholin, CEO of the Center for Neighborhood Technology, a Chicago nonprofit that researches and launches projects with economic and environmental benefits for urban areas, poses with one of the company's I-Go Hybrid Electric Vehicles. *AP Photo/M. Spencer Green*

tasks if the organization is large. The structure of most longstanding, established nonprofit organizations usually consists of a board of directors, committees, staff (including directors), and members or clients. The board of directors will hire the staff director, and the director will report to the board. In small organizations, the director may actually be the person who came up with the idea for, and started, the organization—this director's responsibilities will closely resemble those of an entrepreneur running his or her own business.

Regardless of the size of the organization, a major part of a director's job is fund-raising and promoting the organization. This may be done through grant requests, brainstorming and organizing special events to raise funds, holding membership drives, and partnering with other organizations to host events and programs. Directors help research and identify donors and additional sources of revenue. They also help raise awareness of the organization's

(continues on page 6)

 **INTERVIEW**

Kathryn Cervino
Director, Coastal Preservation Network
College Point, New York

Q. **What inspired you to start this organization, and when was it officially established?**

A. It was 2002, and my husband and I had recently returned to our hometown to live after a few years in the south. We went running in our favorite local park on the waterfront in northeast Queens. As we ran past the water and looked over the edge, we saw how polluted the shoreline was—really just covered with trash, a very depressing sight. We held our first volunteer cleanup a few months later, and the turnout was remarkable. We found that many, many people love this town and are eager to volunteer and help their local environment. They simply didn't know how to get started, and just needed someone to take the lead. It ends up this was the first-ever waterfront cleanup at this city park, and it was the launch of our organization. We ultimately formalized our group and incorporated it as a 501(c)3.

Q. **What steps did you have to take to get started?**

A. First, we needed to establish that there was a need for us—that became evident rather quickly. We created the name "Coastal Preservation Network" using the back-of-the-napkin approach, and began using it to build recognition. We wanted to apply for grants but did not have a 501(c)3 status, so, [we] learned that we needed a "fiscal sponsor." A local nonprofit, in existence for many years in our community, agreed to serve in that capacity. Then, we went about securing an employee ID number and then, our own nonprofit status, so we could do direct fund-raising and grant solicitation. Filing that paperwork is a bit complex, but through the help of a city legal clearinghouse, we were matched with a wonderful attorney in New York who offers his services *pro bono* to small community organizations such as my own. All that in hand, we applied for grants and received our first: a $5,000 grant that enabled us to purchase a variety of important resources for our group. These include: design and printing of our organizational brochure, sea grasses to plant along the shoreline, Web site design and hosting, and several kayaks and related gear to support our water-access initiative.

Q. What day-to-day tasks are involved in directing the organization?

A. There is a lot of communication involved—phone calls, emails, faxes—as we reach out to many other community organizations (civic associations, libraries, churches, ambulance corps), prospective partners and donors, and volunteers. There's outreach to volunteers and media before events to drum up exposure and support. There is extensive communication with parks department personnel—when you're working within park boundaries, you need to secure permits, get clearance for work dates, coordinate for pickup of trash (from cleanup days), etc. There is the graphic artist side as well: making flyers that are eye-catching, photocopying them, and stapling them to telephone poles, handing them out at local merchants, and getting them taped in windows. There is quite a bit of thinking and planning about the next event, how to make it even more successful than the last, and what added element could give it an extra edge. There is creation of thank-you certificates to our donors. And, importantly, there is the continual perusal of grant opportunities, and when great opportunities arise, applying for those grants. There is also meeting with other community players. For example, today I went to a kayaking club in another part of Queens to speak with the boathouse captain, observe their operation, and talk to volunteers to get a feel for how they do it. Our group will be modeling their operation and, if all goes well, offer similar free-kayaking days in our local area. And there is the set-up and break down for events—washing the kayaks, bringing the folding table and chairs to the park, networking with those who show an interest.

(continues)

(continued)

Q. Do you have a staff? Who helps you get the work done, and whom do you work with most closely on projects?

A. At its core this group consists of my husband and me, working to get things done in coordination with the city parks department and its volunteer coordinator arm (called "Partnerships for Parks"). When it comes time for us to host an event, we turn to a few dedicated volunteers and community organizations that are wonderful and always eager to help spread the word and pitch in on tasks. They're great. We've also built relationships with sponsors in the community to gain support for events. Starbucks gives coffee; Home Depot donates supplies (trash bags, gloves, and a water cooler so far); [and] a local restaurant provides pizza for hard-working beach cleaners and sea grass planters. A Queens-based kayaking club is giving us their time and loan of their boats at an upcoming try-a-kayak event we're hosting. So, many people play a role, and we ringmaster while handling tasks as well.

Q. What's your educational and work background?

A. For about seven years I've been a communications manager for health- and environment-related nonprofit organizations

---

(continued from page 3)

cause by doing such things as networking through professional and business associations, holding press conferences, writing and placing articles in the media, participating on speakers' panels at conferences, and speaking at schools and universities. They liaise with other nonprofit and public-sector agencies, government representatives, foundations, community and partner organizations, and businesses. They help create long-range business plans for the organization, as well as contribute to advertising and promotion efforts. Directors also make sure the organization is in compliance with the legal requirements to maintain its nonprofit status by consulting with attorneys and financial and tax specialists, when needed.

Directors handle the human resources side of the business, hiring as well as overseeing and managing employees. They manage and oversee budgets. In smaller organizations they may even be responsible for payroll, accounts receivable and payable, and the (with enviable multimillion-dollar budgets and sizeable staffs, unlike ours). Prior to that I was a journalist for 15 years. I have two master's degrees, in political science and in environmental science, though I don't consider that at all essential for this type of thing.

Q. What tips can you give to students who are interested in this type of work?

A. You just need a passion for whatever it is you're pursuing. That, and perseverance in the face of bureaucracy, will be key to your success. My passion has been to restore our local environment and reconnect people (myself included) with the water. My community is surrounded by water, yet chain-link fences separate us from entering. This barrier shouldn't exist, nor should massive amounts of trash on the beach be accepted as a fact of life. Sometimes, though, it just takes one person to question the status quo, to get the ball rolling toward change.

Q. Are there any books you've read that you can recommend on the topic?

A. *The Riverkeepers*, by John Cronin and Robert F. Kennedy Jr., is completely inspiring.

bookkeeping. They may also be responsible for researching and purchasing office equipment and supplies, and maintaining inventories. Those who own and run their own nonprofit business are generally responsible for securing funding, managing budgets, creating business plans, marketing and promoting the organization, securing members and sponsors and volunteers, and creating and managing events.

REQUIREMENTS
High School

Nonprofit directors need strong communication skills to help them motivate employees and successfully communicate their organization's mission to the general public. While in high school, course work in English, communications, business, math, environmental studies, biology, ecology, history, and computer science will give you a solid background for future green nonprofit work. Fluency in a foreign language is also useful, particularly for future work in an international nonprofit organization.

Postsecondary Training
A bachelor's degree provides a solid foundation for work as a director of a nonprofit green organization. Most organizations prefer advanced degrees coupled with years of nonprofit management experience. Degree majors vary, and can be in any number of subjects—some might be related to the nature of the nonprofit business, such as if the organization is focused on wetland preservation or wildlife conservation, while others will be useful for other components of the business, such as business administration, science, environmental science, environmental policy and law, communications, natural resource management, etc. More schools are now offering degree programs in nonprofit business management as well as in green business management and sustainable business management and administration. While in college, take classes in business management, marketing, communications, public relations, environmental sciences and environmental policy. Sociology and psychology will also help you gain a better understanding of what makes people tick and what keeps them motivated in work and in life.

Most staff executive directors in large nonprofit organizations have graduate degrees, often in business or public administration, some specifically in nonprofit management.

Certification or Licensing
Nonprofit directors can be certified as association executives and professional managers through such organizations as the American Association of Society Executives, the American Management Association, and the Institute of Certified Professional Managers.

Other Requirements
Directors of green nonprofit businesses need to be organized, focused, energetic, decisive, and have strong, clear communication skills. The role is demanding, requiring management skills for internal staff as well as the ability to effectively present the organization's mission to external businesses, the media, and to the general public. Being skilled in the art of persuasion is also crucial for fund-raising work—a big part of most directors' jobs. People skills are required, and diplomacy and leadership abilities are called upon regularly. Knowledge about the green nonprofit business, business trends,

environmental laws and policies, and business management procedures and policies are essential in the job. Physical fitness may also be required for some positions, depending on the nature of the organization.

To keep up with news and stay ahead of the curve in business, directors must be willing to continually learn by participating in conferences, attending workshops, reading books and magazines, and networking regularly with other professionals within the industry as well as in other industries. Directors may work long hours, particularly if they manage smaller organizations. Passion for the cause, dedication to the job, and a flexible schedule are important for success in the job.

EXPLORING

You can find answers to many questions and learn more about what's involved in starting and running a nonprofit organization by reading "The Nonprofit FAQ" at Idealist.org (http://www.idealist.org/npofaq). Publications such as *The Chronicle of Philanthropy* (http://philanthropy.com) and *The NonProfit Times* (http://www.nptimes.com) are good sources of information about news, trends, and issues in the nonprofit sector. Organizations such as the Foundation Center offer a variety of resources—from job listings to classes on how to write grant proposals—for people working in the nonprofit sector and those exploring the field as a possible career. Visit http://foundationcenter.org to learn more. And naturally, another great way to learn more about the field is through internships and volunteer work. You can search for available positions on the Web sites of the organizations that most interest you, as well as by visiting the internship section of Idealist.org (http://www.idealist.org/if/as/Internship).

EMPLOYERS

There are about 402,000 chief executives, including directors, employed in the United States. Directors of green nonprofit organizations work for a variety of charities and foundations. They may work for organizations that focus on land or water preservation, habitat protection, wetland creation or restoration, or groups that provide management and educational services. According to the Bureau of Labor Statistics, the nonprofit sector is steadily growing. In 1994 there were about 1.1 million nonprofit organizations in the United States, employing approximately 5.4 million people. By

2007, the numbers had risen to more than 1.64 million nonprofit institutions, employing 8.7 million workers.

STARTING OUT

For many directors of green nonprofit organizations, career paths are more "organic" than linear. While it is true that some directors may follow a straight line throughout their careers, first securing a degree in nonprofit business management and then working their way up within companies to upper management levels, others arrive at their positions from various backgrounds; they may have years of experience in the corporate world or with government agencies, and thus bring entirely different perspectives to their roles as directors. Visit the Web sites of the organizations you are interested in to learn more about their mission, programs, and current challenges. Look through their job listings to see if anything catches your eye. You can also explore job listings by visiting the Web sites of such organizations as Bridgestar (http://www.bridgestar.org) and the Foundation Center (http://foundationcenter.org).

ADVANCEMENT

Nonprofit directors can advance by honing their management skills or delving into other areas of the nonprofit business by taking classes and workshops. They can move up by taking management positions at larger nonprofit organizations, and with years of experience, by advancing to chief executive positions, if the organization is structured this way. Directors may also secure certification in nonprofit business management, and pursue advanced degrees in business management or environmental-related subjects. Experienced directors may start their own nonprofit businesses and provide consulting services to other organizations and business owners. Directors can also expand their knowledge by sharing their experience with others through teaching and instructing at colleges, universities, and professional schools, and lecturing and participating in panel discussions offered by professional associations.

EARNINGS

Salaries for directors of green nonprofits vary depending upon a number of factors, including the nature of the organization, the organization's budget and source of funding, the size of the organization and the region in which it's located, and the director's level of experience. According to the Department of Labor, nonprofit managers earn wages that are similar to those who work in state government, but are lower on average than those of managers in private industry and local government. Those who work for well-established, longstanding nonprofit organizations that are better funded usually earn higher salaries than those who work for small groups or organizations that have been recently established. The Bureau of Labor Statistics reports that in 2008, annual salaries for general and operations managers were about $91,570, with the lowest paid 10 percent earning $45,410 and the top paid 10 percent averaging $166,400 or higher; chief executives had annual salaries ranging from $68,680 to $166,400. Those who managed companies and enterprises earned about $128,350 per year. Managers of office and administrative support workers had lower annual salaries that ranged from $27,770 for the lowest paid 10 percent, to an average of $45,790 for the middle 50 percent, to $74,640 or more for the top paid 10 percent.

WORK ENVIRONMENT

Directors typically work more than 40 hours per week. Generally, they work in offices, although they may work outdoors occasionally if the organization focuses on an environmental mission such as wetlands management or wildlife habitat preservation. For instance, if they work for preservation groups like Kathryn Cervino's organization, they may spend time hosting kayak demonstrations, paddling around in coastal areas and talking to people about conservation efforts and the ways in which they can get more involved. Directors' schedules vary regularly because they are often the "face" of the organization, and are therefore required to participate in events, meetings, and press conferences. Work hours can stretch into evenings and weekends. Some travel is also involved in the job, especially if directors work for large organizations with national and/or international branches.

OUTLOOK

Continuing interest in environmental issues will drive the need for various green nonprofit services. Although top executives in general will see little or no employment growth through 2016, those who work in professional, scientific, and technical services can look forward to excellent job opportunities, according to the Department of Labor. Competition for positions is expected to be fierce.

Directors with advanced degrees, years of professional experience with successful organizations, and excellent communication and fund-raising skills will fare the best in their hunt for work. Other assets that can be deciding factors in securing director positions in green nonprofit organizations can include foreign language fluency, experience in dealing with the press and various media, solid knowledge of environmental regulations and laws, familiarity with the communities and cultures with which the organization regularly interacts, and ability in marketing, economics, and information systems.

FOR MORE INFORMATION

Find information about educational programs, conferences, certification, and more at

**American Association of Society Executives
and The Center for Association Leadership**
1575 I Street, NW
Washington, DC 20005-1105
Tel: 888-950-2723
http://www.asaecenter.org

To learn more about membership, seminars, publications, and certification, contact

American Management Association
1601 Broadway
New York, NY 10019-7434
Tel: 877-566-9441
Email: customerservice@amanet.org
http://www.amanet.org

Learn more about this organization's activities by visiting its Web site at

Coastal Preservation Network
http://www.coastalpreservation.org

Find nonprofit job listings and other resources at

The Foundation Center
79 Fifth Avenue, 16th Street
New York, NY 10003-3076
Tel: 212-620-4230
http://foundationcenter.org

For information about professional management certification, contact
Institute of Certified Professional Managers
James Madison University, MSC 5504
Harrisonburg, VA 22807-0002
Tel: 800-568-4120
http://www.icpm.biz

For information about educational forums, conferences, and networking opportunities, contact
National Management Association
2210 Arbor Boulevard
Dayton, OH 45439-1506
Tel: 937-294-0421
Email: nma@nmal.org
http://nmal.org

Find governmental information about nonprofit businesses and useful resources at
USA.gov for Nonprofits
http://www.usa.gov/Business/Nonprofit.shtml

Directors of Volunteers, Green Nonprofit Organizations

OVERVIEW

Directors of volunteers manage volunteer programs for green nonprofit groups such as conservation organizations, and wildlife societies and foundations. They plan volunteer programs and identify volunteer roles, suggest policies for volunteer involvement, write volunteer job descriptions, recruit volunteers and conduct orientations, train staff members in how to work with volunteers, assess programs and write reports, and create and manage budgets.

HISTORY

In 2008 about 61.8 million people in the United States—that's 26.4 percent of the population—volunteered at least once through or for a nonprofit organization, according to the Bureau of Labor Statistics. In spite of the recent recession, volunteer rates have remained fairly stable over the past few years. There has been an increase in alternative forms of volunteering, such as in Americans working more collaboratively with their neighbors (up 31 percent in 2008, compared to the previous year). Also, more young people are volunteering: in 2008, 8.2 million young adults (ages 16-24) volunteered, a 5.7 percent increase over the 7.8 million volunteers in this age bracket in 2007.

People volunteer for many reasons—for example, to make a difference, to learn new skills, or to meet new people. Those who volunteer for green nonprofit organizations are committed to helping improve the environment and educating others about conservation, renewable energy sources, and other "green" topics. Volunteer directors ensure that the volunteer experience is rewarding and meaningful by creating interesting programs and matching people to work that makes the most sense for their abilities and interests.

THE JOB

Volunteers are the muscle behind the activities of green nonprofit organizations. Volunteer programs are important for attracting people who want to be actively involved in helping the organization further its mission and meet goals—whether by making phone calls to help raise funds or pitching in on a park clean-up day. Volunteer programs are also important for involving families in conservation and environmental activities, helping parents and kids learn together about environmental issues and the steps they can take at home and in their everyday lives to help improve things.

Volunteer directors are, in a way, human resource managers. Their work involves recruiting volunteers and overseeing their work. They are also the representatives of the organization that members and prospective members often meet first and get to know the best. First impressions of an organization are often made through initial contact with the volunteer manager. Effective volunteer directors are well versed in the organization and passionate and enthusiastic about its cause. These qualities are critical in the job because they are contagious; enthusiasm causes intrigue and the desire to learn more. Volunteer directors are able to explain all aspects of the organization's mission, philosophies, activities, and staff structure in ways that educate and engage people.

Directors create volunteer programs to keep current members as well as attract new members. The programs are designed to educate people about the organization while making use of their skills and expertise. The arrangement is mutually beneficial: Volunteers feel personally rewarded for their contributions, and they can also enhance certain skills and expand knowledge through volunteer work; organizations save money through volunteer work and also generate good will and improve their image in communities through volunteer programs and achievement of goals.

Other aspects of volunteer directors' jobs include evaluating the organization's need for volunteers in certain areas, writing proposals for volunteer programs (including projected outcomes), and creating all of the materials needed for the programs (including applications, volunteer agreements, orientation handbooks, as well as volunteer policies and procedures). Directors also maintain databases of volunteers and volunteer statistics. They work with senior managers and board members on strategic planning, and often work closely with other departments such as development, marketing, and public relations on fund-raising and membership outreach projects. In larger organizations volunteer directors hire and manage staff, such as *volunteer managers* and *volunteer coordinators*, to help them coordinate and manage volunteer programs.

REQUIREMENTS
High School
Classes that provide a good foundation for volunteer management work in green nonprofit organizations include earth science, biology, ecology, environmental studies (if offered in your school), English, math, history, and computers.

Postsecondary Training
Undergraduate degrees vary for directors of volunteers positions. Some directors have bachelor's or master's degrees in nonprofit business management, which includes course work in grant writing and fund-raising. Others may have teaching degrees, or degrees in English or communications. A variety of backgrounds are suitable to volunteer management work, as long as the individual has requisite management and people skills, and an appreciation and passion for the organization. In general, classes that provide useful knowledge for the job include marketing and advertising, business management, communications, public relations, psychology, social science, and environmental studies.

Other Requirements
Directors of volunteers have strong written and oral communication skills and enjoy working with a wide variety of people, from

volunteers and local community members, to staff, board members, and the general public. Diplomacy and cultural sensitivity are essential in the job. The ability to connect with people, fully understand their skills and talents, and match them to appropriate volunteer work is a large part of the job. Directors of volunteers have good intuition about people. Strong leadership skills are required, as are conflict management abilities. If a volunteer is not acting according to the organization's rules of conduct, it's up to directors to know when to intervene and when to "fire" a volunteer. Volunteer directors need to be multitaskers who are organized, detail-oriented, and able to work independently as well as on teams. Knowledge of Microsoft Office and other software programs, including volunteer recruitment software, is also required.

EXPLORING

Learn more about volunteer management careers by visiting the Volunteer Management Resource Center on Idealist.org (http://www.idealist.org/en/vmrc). Search the site for tips on how to start your own volunteer program and find information about professional development in the field (such as conferences, workshops, and online training opportunities). Other useful sites to explore for volunteer management projects and ideas are Volunteer Match (http://www.volunteermatch.org) and Volunteering in America (http://www.volunteeringinamerica.gov).

EMPLOYERS

Directors of volunteers for green nonprofit organizations work for environmental and conservation groups, schools, and consultancies. They may work for organizations that provide services such as public interest research, wildlife conservation, outdoor education and recreation, and environmental protection and advocacy. They work for foundations, charitable organizations, and nonprofit groups and programs that may be established by corporations and for-profit businesses.

STARTING OUT

Volunteering or interning with a green nonprofit organization provides you the opportunity to do good deeds while gaining exposure to the field. Energize, Inc., an international training, consulting, and publishing firm specializing in volunteerism, provides various resources for managers of volunteers and students who are interested in pursuing careers in volunteer management. Visit their Web site (http://www.energizeinc.com) to learn more about job and internship postings, "hot topics" about the field, upcoming events, workshops, and e-newsletters.

ADVANCEMENT

Volunteer directors who work for large organizations may advance by managing the volunteer programs of other regions within the organization. They may also move up by taking senior positions within other departments of the organization, where their recruitment and management skills are much needed. They may also advance by securing advanced degrees in nonprofit business management, or by writing, teaching, and lecturing. Salaried volunteer directors can also advance by starting their own nonprofit organizations and consulting businesses.

EARNINGS

Salaries for directors of volunteers vary based on level of experience and the organization's budget. SimplyHired.com reports $55,000 as the average annual income for managers of volunteer programs in 2009, although this number does not specify industry sector. The organization People First reports in its 2008 "Global Volunteer Management Survey" that the average yearly income for volunteer managers was $45,296, with annual salaries for full-time managers starting as low as $9,600 and ranging to $90,000 or higher. Of those surveyed, 67 percent had been working in their job for less than five years; 9 percent worked for education and research organizations, 5 percent for environmental groups, and 2 percent for animal welfare.

The U.S. Department of Labor (DoL) does not yet report on salary information for directors of volunteers. The job closest to volunteer management in overall responsibilities and skills required that DoL shows statistics for is human resources, training, and labor specialist. In 2008 these specialists earned average annual incomes ranging from $27,980 to $93,880.

Volunteer directors usually receive employment benefits in addition to salaries, which can include health insurance, paid holidays and vacations, personal time off, and retirement plans.

WORK ENVIRONMENT

Volunteer directors spend their time working in offices as well as working on site where volunteers work. If the organization focuses on outdoor projects, directors may be needed to supervise volunteers in action and coordinate activities. Work hours are generally 40 hours per week, but directors may need to work evenings or weekends if deadlines are approaching for projects or if volunteer events are scheduled after business hours.

OUTLOOK

Volunteer directors should have good employment opportunities in the next few years. Interest in environmental issues and sustainable business practices continues to grow and more nonprofit companies in the "green" sector will turn to volunteer programs as ways to help them increase membership and achieve specific goals. The U.S. Department of Labor predicts that demand for services offered by advocacy, grant-making, and civic organizations will be on the rise through at least 2016. Many jobs will also become available as volunteer directors leave positions for other jobs or retire from the field.

FOR MORE INFORMATION

More than 84,000 nonprofit organizations from more than 180 countries have created profiles and listed information about their missions and opportunities on Idealist.org. Find postings for volunteer, intern, and paid positions, as well as other resources by visiting

Action Without Borders/Idealist.org
302 Fifth Avenue, 11th Floor
New York, NY 10001-3604
http://www.idealist.org

Find information about membership, committees, events, and workshops by visiting the Web sites of the following associations:

**American Association of Society Executives
and The Center for Association Leadership**
1575 I Street, NW
Washington, DC 20005-1105
Tel: 888-950-2723
http://www.asaecenter.org

Association of Leaders in Volunteer Engagement
PO Box 465
South Paris, ME 04281-0465
Email: info@volunteeralive.org
http://www.volunteeralive.org

Find career information, publications, and networking opportunities in volunteer management by visiting

Energize, Inc.
5450 Wissahickon Avenue
Philadelphia, PA 19144-5221
Tel: 215-438-8342
http://www.energizeinc.com

Find statistics about volunteering and other resources by visiting the following Web site:

Volunteering in America
http://www.volunteeringinamerica.gov

Ecomanagers, Green Hotels/Resorts

OVERVIEW

Ecomanagers of green hotels and resorts oversee all aspects of resorts, hotels, inns, and other accommodations that are eco-friendly. Resorts, hotels, and other accommodations qualify for this designation if they use features such as wind and solar power, have strict recycling programs, and display other sustainable practices. Ecomanagers hire and oversee all staff, including housekeeping, kitchen, and wait staff; grounds maintenance; public relations; and reservations. They are also responsible for planning, developing, and promoting marketing programs, and managing the resort's finances.

HISTORY

Traveling into nature to escape everyday stress and reconnect with the environment is an old pastime. It was especially favored in the 1800s and early 1900s by wealthy families such as Albany businessman Robert Pruyn, who built the Santanoni Lodge, one of the first "great camps" (a series of numerous houses and structures established over a wide swath of open land) in the Adirondacks. People still flock to nature for their getaways, but many are also signing up for trips that have lighter effects on the environment and feature conservation, local community, and/ or environmental action projects in which they can participate. This type of environmentally conscious travel is known as eco-tourism. It's a term that was introduced to the *Merriam-Webster Dictionary* in 1982, but did not really become part of our vernacular until the past five to 10 years. According to a *Forbes Traveler* article by Stephen Regenold ("Luxury Eco-Resorts '08," April 18, 2008), ecotourism is "More than a trend . . . there are now thousands of ecologically oriented lodges in more than 60 countries around the planet."

THE JOB

Ecomanagers are responsible for the smooth operations of resorts that are environmentally friendly. Eco-resorts are located anywhere in the world, from jungles and forests, to coastal areas and mountainsides. Managers may work for resorts located in privately owned forest preserves, such as Elk Lake Lodge in the Adirondacks, or in coastal and tropical areas, such as Maho Bay in the Virgin Islands. Regardless of the location, ecomanagers' core responsibilities remain the same: Their job is to manage all departments and oversee all aspects of the resort. In smaller organizations, they may be involved in hiring, training, and supervising staff. They may also be more directly, and actively, involved in other areas, such as working with ground maintenance crews to maintain hiking trails and clear roads of debris.

Ecomanagers direct and oversee the refurbishment of existing structures and construction of new structures. This may involve interviewing and contracting building engineers, construction workers, or even landscape architects. They make sure that the materials and structures being planned are eco-friendly (e.g., wood reused from previous structures), and that work being done at the site meets governmental safety regulations. Many eco-resorts are built to be in harmony with nature and to make the best use of it without causing damage. For instance, Maho Bay features elevated walkways so as not to cause soil erosion and hand-construction methods that left the natural environment completely undisturbed.

Managing the resort's budget and finances is also part of an eco-manager's job. They create budgets; approve expenditures; and contract professional services, such as accounting and tax preparations. Sustainability projects and programs are factored into budgets as well. Other aspects of the job include expanding marketing and promotion efforts by strategizing new features that can be added to the resort to either attract more guests or tap into a new target market. Examples may be offering wireless Internet service to guests, using only locally produced food, or providing complementary chemical-free and biodegradable bathing products in the rooms. Ecomanagers also hold staff meetings to discuss sustainability and conservation efforts at the resort, and to guide staff in how to communicate these developments and features with guests. Ecomanagers invite staff to contribute thoughts and ideas about how the resort can become more eco-friendly and efficient.

Eco-resort managers may also be couples who work in teams to manage the resort, each handling the parts of the job in which they are strongest. A 2009 job advertisement for an eco-resort manager was seeking an individual or couple with five years' prior experience to manage a 38-unit resort in the Caribbean that included a general store, café, pool, and event pavilion. The job required direct involvement with staffing, training, and motivating and supporting various departments such as registration, bookkeeping, budgeting, maintenance, housekeeping, security, the retail store, activities, and food service. The resort preferred individuals with experience in ecotourism, hospitality management, and knowledge of the local area. Enthusiastic, versatile, resilient, and hands-on people with strong work ethics were encouraged to reply. The resort's hilly terrain and numerous steps required physically fit applicants who could handle the tropical climate while running around. Housing or a housing allowance was also a possible offer, and the salary started at $35,000 and included benefits.

Customer service is all-important in this type of work. Ecomanagers ensure that all guest, staff, and facility needs are met and that customers' complaints are handled diplomatically and constructively. They oversee the services that will be offered to guests, including housekeeping, dining options, and dining and meeting facilities. Many eco-resorts offer educational programs and outdoor activities. Ecomanagers ensure that guides or teachers who are brought in from outside the organization to lead activities for guests are qualified to do the job and have a good reputation in the field.

(continues on page 26)

 **INTERVIEW**

Mike Sheridan
Lodge Manager, Elk Lake Lodge
North Hudson, New York

Q. What are some of the things you're doing to make Elk Lake greener? What's required for this designation?

A. We are fortunate with our relatively small size (54-person maximum occupancy) to be able to concentrate on nearly all aspects of conservation—from simply sort-separating all garbage and recyclables to more involved replacement of all existing septic waste systems with cleaner, more efficient leach fields. We purchase local produce when available, use 100 percent recycled paper in our office, and have switched all of our exterior stains from oil to water base. There are many ways to be environmentally conscious, but we feel that by looking at the simplest ways to conserve we are doing our part to be as "green" as possible. We have also been accepted into the Audubon Green Leaf Eco-Rating Program for Hotels, which is a comprehensive guide to industry standards for environmental stewardship.

Q. What are your main responsibilities in your job as lodge manager?

A. My responsibilities range from flipping eggs to running a chain saw. Elk Lake Lodge is a 12,000-acre private wilderness preserve with 40 miles of maintained hiking trails; two lakes supporting brook trout, landlocked salmon, and lake trout; eight cabins; a six-room lodge with a complete dining room; and a staff of 17. I'm responsible for the maintenance and upkeep of the preserve and structures, and the management of our staff.

Q. What sparked your interest in this type of work?

A. I've worked in the service industry since 1989 when I finished my enlistment in the army and moved to Lake Placid, New York. I've been fortunate to have had jobs that helped to shape my career and teach me about the outdoor industry, from waiting tables to outdoor retail sales to ski patrolling. The job that most solidified my career choice was working as an interior caretaker in the High Peaks Wilderness Area, which eventually led me to Elk Lake as a caretaker and eventually as manager.

Q. What do you love most about your job?

A. What I love most is that every day is different and there are always challenges on every level. I'm able to perform different jobs without the tasks becoming monotonous—from running heavy equipment or a sawmill, to carpentry, plumbing, and welding. I get to help with the kitchen, run the front desk, and work with our bookkeeper. I'm lucky enough to be able to do so many interesting, challenging, and fun jobs without them becoming tedious. Also, I get to meet so many interesting people who have a common thread in loving the outdoors and what Elk Lake has to offer.

Q. What has surprised you the most about the work, or the field?

A. . . . [That] I'm able to have the job that I have, and to know that when the work gets tough, I just need to go outside, smell the fresh air, take in the amazing scenery, and realize how fortunate I am to be able to work in a green industry.

Q. What book can you recommend that really inspired you?

A. Anything by Farley Mowatt, especially *Never Cry Wolf.* It taught me to not assume anything about nature and to realize that the environment is a very fragile system.

Q. Any tips you can share for students interested in this field?

A. My advice is to study and read about the natural sciences. This will give you an appreciation for working in and around nature and the outdoors. Also, there are many outdoor and conservation organizations that appreciate volunteerism. These programs can be fun, from trail work to wildlife rehabilitation.

(continued from page 23)

REQUIREMENTS

High School

Eco-resort managers need strong management skills, knowledge of the environment and wildlife, and the ability to communicate with people from different backgrounds and cultures. Classes that will help in these areas are earth and physical sciences, zoology and ecology (if offered at your school), environmental studies, math, English, computer science, and foreign language.

Postsecondary Training

An associate's degree may be sufficient for some eco-resort manager positions. A bachelor's degree, however, may boost chances for employment. Many different degrees are useful for eco-resort management work, including environmental science and studies, engineering, wildlife science, or business management. More schools are offering degree programs in ecotourism. Course work useful to this type of job generally includes natural resource management, sustainability, hotel and resort management, tourism analysis, international tourism, environmental science, cultural anthropology, psychology, marketing, math, English, and computer software and database programs.

Certification or Licensing

Ecomanagers can enhance their careers and business knowledge by securing resort management certification from hotel or lodging associations such as the American Hotel and Lodging Educational Institute (http://www.ei-ahla.org).

Other Requirements

Skills required in this job include leadership and management abilities, strong and clear verbal and written communication skills, ability to manage and mentor employees and delegate responsibilities when needed, decision-making skills, along with physical fitness and stamina. Diplomacy and professionalism are required for interactions with staff, visitors, management, and the general public. Passion for the environment and wildlife, and solid knowledge of conservation and sustainable resort operations are also needed.

EXPLORING

Read travel magazines and visit travel Web sites to learn about developments in the ecotourism field. Check out *Green Lodging News* (http://www.greenlodgingnews.com) for updates on eco-resorts and ecotourism. Other useful resources can be found at the International Ecotourism Society's Web site (http://www.ecotourism.org). The American Hotel and Lodging Association and the International Council on Hotel, Restaurant, and Institutional Education offer hospitality management training programs. (Contact information is located at the end of this article.)

EMPLOYERS

Eco-resort managers work for lodges, hotels, motels, and other businesses that provide accommodations for environmentally conscious travelers. They may also own the resort themselves. According to the U.S. Department of Labor, there were 71,000 lodging managers employed in 2006. More than half were self-employed, mainly as small hotel and bed-and-breakfast inn owners.

STARTING OUT

Get a part-time job in the reservation department, or any other department, of an eco-resort. This will give you the opportunity to see how the resort is run and the various types of programs and features that are offered. Talk with the manager and learn more about how he or she got started in the field. Find out what their educational background is and where they worked beforehand. You can also use the Internet to explore eco-resorts and contact managers to see about setting up information interviews by visiting such Web sites as Eco Tropical Resorts (http://www.eco-tropicalresorts.com) and EcoClub Ecotourism Directory (http://www.ecoclub.com/lodges.html).

ADVANCEMENT

Ecomanagers who work for large organizations may advance through the company's ranks to more senior management positions, overseeing more resorts in different regions and managing more departments and employees. Advancement may come from introducing new programs, structures, or functions that improve the resort's operations and elevate it to higher levels of sustainability. Honing management skills, learning more about sustainable practices and operations, and sharing knowledge with staff and customers are other ways ecomanagers advance in their field. Managers may progress by taking on other aspects of the business, such as writing newsletters for the resort's Web site or organizing and leading workshops about eco-resort and environmental issues.

EARNINGS

The Bureau of Labor Statistics (BLS) does not show statistics specific to ecomanagers, but reports that lodging managers averaged about $45,800 per year in 2008; the lowest paid 10 percent earned annual incomes of $28,160 and the top paid 10 percent averaged $84,270 or higher. Managers' salaries vary depending on years of experience. For example, resort managers with one to four years of experience earned median salaries ranging from $27,710 to $46,915 in 2009, according to Payscale.com. Those with five to 10 years of experience averaged $41,221 to $60,226 annually, and resort managers who had 10 to 19 years of professional experience earned $46,160 to $73,560 per year. Those with expertise in certain areas of eco-resort management, strong knowledge of conservation and sustainable operations, and familiarity with the local community have better chances of commanding higher incomes. Depending on the resort, ecomanagers may also be offered on-site housing or housing discounts along with salary and benefits such as health care and paid holidays.

WORK ENVIRONMENT

An ecomanager's work is never done. They often start their days early and end late in the evenings. They also work weekends and are on call 24/7 in case emergencies arise and they are needed to resolve problems. The ability to evaluate problems and make effective decisions quickly is paramount in this line of work. Ecomanagers are also on-site for resort events such as weddings, and may work particularly hectic hours during peak travel seasons and during seasonal openings and closures of the resort.

OUTLOOK

Employment opportunities for general resort managers is expected to grow about as fast as the average for all occupations through 2016, according to the Department of Labor. Increased domestic and foreign travel, and steady business travel will drive growth. Interest in sustainable travel and green destinations is also continuing to grow. More eco-resorts are opening every year and will need managers to oversee operations. Competition is expected to be keen, however, as many of these jobs are in interesting locations, providing managers with opportunities to work in unique, natural settings. Typically, the number of applicants far outweighs the available positions. A college degree, previous eco-resort management experience, and special skills and knowledge can boost a candidate's chance for the job.

FOR MORE INFORMATION

Learn more about hospitality training programs and find publications and other resources for travel industry professionals by visiting

American Hotel and Lodging Association
1201 New York Avenue, NW, Suite 600
Washington, DC 20005-3931
Tel: 202-289-3100
http://www.ahla.com

Learn more about ecotourism projects and find news and events at

Center for Responsible Travel
1333 H Street, NW, Suite 300, East Tower
Washington, DC 20005-4707
Tel: 202-347-9203
http://www.responsibletravel.org

Find information about careers, scholarships, and upcoming conferences by visiting

International Council on Hotel, Restaurant, and Institutional Education
2810 North Parham Road, Suite 230
Richmond, VA 23294-4422
Tel: 804-346-4800
http://www.chrie.org

Learn more about ecotourism in action by visiting Maho Bay's Web site at

Maho Bay
PO Box 310, Cruz Bay
Saint John, VI 00830-0310
Tel: 800-392-9004
Email: MahoBay@Maho.org
http://maho.org

Ecotourism Agents/Planners

OVERVIEW

Ecotourism agents and planners research and recommend trips to people who are concerned about the environment and want to travel to destinations where they can experience nature and help support local cultures. Ecotourism agents and planners research destinations to ensure that conservation practices are promoted there and that natural settings and wildlife are continuously preserved and protected. They also make sure that local governments support environmental conservation efforts and that the political, economic, and social climates of destinations are safe for ecotravelers. Agents and planners are also responsible for handling transportation and hotel bookings and confirmations.

HISTORY

"Leave smaller footprints" has become the tagline for a relatively new sector in the travel industry: ecotourism. The World Conservation Union and The Nature Conservancy have adopted the following definition of ecotourism: "Environmentally responsible travel to natural areas, in order to enjoy and appreciate nature (and accompanying cultural features, both past and present) that promote conservation, have a low visitor impact and provide for beneficially active socio-economic involvement of local peoples." The Nature Conservancy points out that ecotourism is distinctly different from nature tourism as it is not simply about a trip into the great outdoors, but rather sustainable travel that emphasizes conservation, traveler responsibility, and active community participation.

Ecotourism consists of sensitivity toward and appreciation of biodiversity and local cultures; visitor behavior that is conscientious and has low impact; support for local conservation efforts and sustainable benefits to local communities; local participation in decision making; and educational aspects for travelers as well as local communities.

THE JOB

Ecotourism agents and planners help adventurous travelers find trips in the outdoors that are educational, awareness raising, and environmentally friendly. Some ecotravelers prefer to study animals, while others are more interested in geology and landscapes. Types of activities people seek in ecotourism include exploring and hiking in natural parks, canyons, and volcanoes; visiting and studying certain aspects of tropical rainforests; whale-watching trips; and small group trips (in "green" ships) to the Arctic Circle. Other activities may include camping, biking, horseback riding, and kayaking and canoeing. Ecotravel may also be to nonexotic places as well, such as cities and areas that are environmentally aware and active in conservation efforts. Agents help customers find and book rooms at hotels, inns, and other resorts and accommodations that either have "green hotel" designations or are structured in ways to have minimal impact on the environment.

Ecotourism agents and planners meet with clients to discuss trip ideas and learn the types of activities and projects in which they want to participate during their travels. To recommend destinations to clients, ecotourism agents and planners conduct surveys of clients who have already visited the sites, review online testimonials that visitors have posted on Internet travel sites or on the destination's Web site itself, and read articles and books about the areas. Agents and planners look for accommodations that are not newly constructed, or they look for those that are harmonious with the environment, such as huts and tents. Agents and planners also need to know local guides in order to arrange guided tours and outings for visitors, and have awareness of local regulations and rules for visitors.

More people are becoming interested in traveling to green destinations, helping local communities during their travels, and

An ecotourism agent discusses travel options with a client. *Leah-Anne Thompson/Shutterstock Images*

experiencing local culture and learning from the trip. They are educating themselves about conservation projects and ways to get involved. A more educated customer means that ecotourism agents and planners need to be sharp and up to speed on current and upcoming conservation projects. They may keep up with conservation projects and programs by reading conservation magazines and visiting Web sites such as Planeta (http://www.planeta.com), which provides resources and forums for responsible travelers and ecotourism professionals.

Agents/planners handle all aspects of customers' trips, including booking airline, train, and boat tickets; car, scooter, bicycle, boat rentals; travel insurance; hotel reservations; guided tours; and meal packages. They provide maps and reservation confirmations and city information to customers. They are knowledgeable about document requirements for various countries and inform clients about political situations or health risks that may arise or exist in certain areas. Ecotourism agents/planners may work on staff for travel agencies or operate their own ecotourism businesses. They may promote their services at industry conferences and trade shows, as well as through slide presentations to various organizations and educational institutions. They may sell their services directly to individuals, businesses, and through host agencies and ecotravel associations.

REQUIREMENTS
High School
Course work in math, science, geology, history, social science, English, computer science, and foreign language provides a solid foundation for ecotourism agent work.

Postsecondary Training
There are no education requirements for ecotourism careers. More schools, however, are offering programs in ecotourism to meet growing demand in this area. Classes that are immediately useful in the job are environmental studies, conservation, cultural studies, political science, communications, English, business, and advertising.

Certification or Licensing
Certification is voluntary and can improve an ecotourism agent's marketability. The Travel Institute (http://www.thetravelinstitute.com) offers certification programs to travel industry professionals. The Sustainable Tourism Certification Network of the Americas

provides a list of programs for sustainable tourism certification on its Web site (http://www.certificationnetwork.org).

Other Requirements

Strong communication skills are required to attract and maintain clients, and also to communicate with ecotourism destinations and companies in other regions and countries. Solid sales and negotiation skills are needed. Knowledge of computer and Internet technology is also required. Attention to detail and the ability to organize massive amounts of information are crucial. Ecotourism agents and planners collect data from a variety of sources and then compare information to help clients create itineraries at prices within their budgets. Ecotourism agents/planners who work for corporate clients must be fast-thinking and able to accommodate last-minute requests, including travel date and flight changes. Business travelers' schedules can change frequently due to spontaneous work requirements, and ecotourism agents/planners must be flexible and adaptable if they want to continue doing business with them. Another asset for ecotourism agents and planners to have is personal travel experience, which helps them understand the many facets involved in arranging travel. Appreciation for other cultures and fluency in other languages are also equally valuable in the job. Strong knowledge of sustainability practices, conservation issues, and environmental studies are important, particularly for conversing and developing rapport with clientele who are themselves environmentally aware and knowledgeable.

EXPLORING

Ecotourism agents/planners depend on a wide range of knowledge to be successful in their jobs. They need to understand not only the business of travel and tourism, but also environmental issues of different regions, cultural mores and practices, and the status of political and economic climates in other countries. One easy way to start gathering information for this career is to read travel and business magazines, everything from *The Economist* to *Travel & Leisure*, as well as environmental and nature magazines such as *National Geographic* and *Audubon*. You can also learn more about the topics ecotravel professionals are discussing by visiting the Center for Sustainable Destinations at National Geographic's Web site (http://www.nationalgeographic.com/travel/sustainable/professionals.html).

You can also learn more about ecotourism by taking a trip yourself. If you can afford to get away for a week or two, you can travel as a "voluntour"—volunteering to help local conservation efforts or other community projects and development initiatives, and getting some time off to tour the area and take in the sites. Planeterra, for example, offers voluntourism projects such as sea turtle conservation projects in Costa Rica that need volunteers for beach patrols. Learn more about sustainable travel and voluntourism by visiting Planeterra's Web site (http://www.planeterra.org). Another great resource is the American Society of Travel Agents' booklet *Becoming a Travel Agent*, which you can find at http://www.asta.org.

EMPLOYERS

Ecotourism agents and planners work for travel agencies, travel departments within corporations and nonprofit organizations, and are also self-employed. They may advise corporate travelers about sustainable, team-building trips for groups, and/or map out travel plans for individuals who are interested in volunteering on conservation projects. The Bureau of Labor Statistics reports that about 101,000 travel agents worked throughout the United States in 2006, and nearly two-thirds of them were employed by travel agencies.

STARTING OUT

Volunteering or working part time for an ecotourism agency is the best way to start out in this field. You can find agents listed on the Ecotour Directory Web site (http://www.ecotourdirectory.com). You can also find job listings by visiting such employment sites as EcoClub.com (http://www.ecoclub.com/jobs/) and Ecotourism Jobs (http://wwwecotourismjobs.org).

Another great way to get a head-start is by joining professional associations for travel agents and attending workshops and conferences. Organizations that offer educational and networking opportunities, among other resources, include the U.S. Travel Association (http://www.tia.org) and the American Society of Travel Agents (http://www.asta.org).

ADVANCEMENT

Ecotourism agents/planners may advance by becoming certified travel agents. Those who work for travel agencies may advance to more senior positions as managers and department heads.

Self-employed ecotourism agents and planners may expand their business by hiring more staff members and opening branches in other regions. Advancement can also come about through lecturing about ecotourism, and writing articles for industry publications as well as conservation literature and Web sites.

EARNINGS

Salaries for ecotourism agents are similar to those of travel coordinators and travel agents. Salary.com reports that median annual incomes for travel coordinators in 2009 were $44,176, with salaries ranging from $31,207 to $55,917 or higher. According to postings on Monster.com, an entry-level travel agent position for a travel agency based in California paid an annual salary of $27,000, and a Utah-based travel agency offered travel agents a salary range of $25,000 to $50,000, depending upon level of experience. According to the U.S. Bureau of Labor Statistics, in 2008 annual salaries for travel agents ranged from $18,770 or less to $47,860 or more, with median earnings of $30,570.

Salaried ecotourism agents and planners may also enjoy benefits such as bonuses and commissions, health insurance, paid vacation and holidays, personal days and sick time, disability, and 401(k) and pension plans.

WORK ENVIRONMENT

Ecotourism agents/planners generally work 40 hours per week in offices. Hours may sometimes be longer if they need to have telephone conversations or exchange emails with people who are in time zones that differ from theirs. They spend some time traveling to meetings and conferences, and may also spend time traveling to destinations to conduct their own reviews before recommending trips to customers.

OUTLOOK

Ecotourism is on the rise. More people are seeking meaningful travel experiences where they can contribute to conservation efforts while learning more about ecosystems, wildlife and plant species, and local cultures of certain regions. The Bureau of Labor Statistics (BLS) does not yet report on ecotourism because it is an emerging sector of the travel industry, but it does show that employment opportunities for travel agents in general will experience little change through

2016. Those with more years of experience and qualifications will fare the best in the job market. And those who specialize in certain niches of travel, such as luxury travel or ecotourism, will find more employment opportunities. Ecotourism agents/planners who have personal travel experience to and strong knowledge of certain destinations, coupled with excellent communication and sales skills, will be in high demand by travelers who seek expert advice on ecotourism trips.

FOR MORE INFORMATION

Learn more about membership and upcoming networking events by visiting

American Society of Travel Agents
1101 King Street, Suite 200
Alexandria, VA 22314-2963
Email: askasta@asta.org
http://www.asta.org

Find job listings in ecotourism and other resources at

ECOCLUB.com
Ecotourism Job Centre
http://www.ecoclub.com/jobs

This organization believes in "the power of travel to transform people and inspire change." Find ecotourism destinations and volunteer opportunities at

The International Ecotourism Society
PO Box 96503, #34145
Washington, DC 20090-6503
Tel: 202-506-5033
Email: membership@ecotourism.org
http://www.ecotourism.org

Find industry news and publications by visiting

U.S. Travel Association
1100 New York Avenue, NW, Suite 450
Washington, DC 20005-3934
Tel: 202-408-8422
http://www.tia.org

Environmental Activists

OVERVIEW

Environmental activists raise awareness about environmental issues through a variety of activities, including door-to-door and street campaigns, and fund-raising and membership drives. They work for private and public environmental groups, helping them create and implement outreach campaigns to further their cause. Activists may also be involved in recruiting and training other activists and supporters.

HISTORY

Benjamin Franklin was an early "public rights" advocate against industrial pollution. At the turn of the 17th century, slaughterhouses and tanneries were dumping their waste (e.g., rotting animal parts, hair, and horns) into Philadelphia's commercial district and a nearby creek. Disease spread through Philadelphia as a result, and fish in the creek died. Residents petitioned the Pennsylvania Assembly to have the tanneries and slaughterhouses moved outside of town, but nothing changed and the dumping continued. It was Franklin's front-page article in his publication, the *Pennsylvania Gazette*, in 1739—advocating for the right to "breathe freely" in one's own house—that finally triggered response and curtailed the dumping.

Keeping the West wild and conserving natural resources was the focus of U.S. naturalists and environmentalists in the 1800s. John Muir was an early proponent of this cause, committing his work and life to studying nature and advocating for its protection and preservation. He raised awareness and educated people about environmental issues through his books, essays, and lobbying efforts. Considered to be the founder of the conservation movement, for years he fought for Yosemite Valley and its surrounding area to be protected. Agriculture, mining, and forestry activities were starting to take their toll on Yosemite's environment, and Muir campaigned tirelessly to prevent development and overuse of that natural area. His efforts eventually paid off: In 1890 Congress designated Yosemite a National Park. Muir went on to found the Sierra Club in 1892, an organization of activists and advocates that continues today with the mission "to explore, enjoy, and protect the wild places of the earth; to practice and promote the responsible use of the earth's ecosystems and resources; to educate and enlist humanity to protect and restore the quality of the natural and human environment; and to use all lawful means to carry out these objectives."

Environmental activism continued to grow in the 20th century, with people rallying around issues such as land conservation and wildlife protection. Ecologists Aldo Leopold and Rachel Carson wrote books that introduced the general public to the idea of being responsible stewards of the planet by treating the environment with respect and responsibility. Numerous environmental groups have formed and grown since then, focused on a variety of environmental issues, from deforestation and habitat wildlife conservation, to air or water pollution, renewable energy sources, recycling and reusing materials, among a host of other topics. Approaches to activism also vary widely, ranging from peaceful resistance, such as the tree-hugging done by environmental activists in the 1970s, to more radical actions, like Earth Liberation Front's tactic of setting fires to the properties of organizations it believes are harming the environment, animals, or people. Today's mainstream environmental activist groups rely on educating people about issues through direct dialogue, social media, and other communications tools. The environmental activist field has become more professionalized since its early days, and depends on educated, specially trained activists to help solve environmental problems.

THE JOB

Environmental activists work on campaigns to raise awareness about environmental issues and to increase membership to and financial support of the organization. They are usually the frontline workers, helping to champion the organization's cause. Other job titles for activists may be *campaign coordinators, outreach coordinators,* and *community outreach coordinators.* Environmental groups use "canvassing" tactics in their campaigns, which include calling people on the phone, paying door-to-door visits, and approaching people on the streets. Activists may do any one or all of these things combined to secure support from local community residents and to develop relationships with relevant agencies such as environmental or public health groups, private and public businesses, civic leaders and public officials, and other individuals and groups that can lend assistance and support to the cause.

Local grassroots activists can often be found out in the streets talking to people about issues. Armed with brochures and clipboards, they work to engage people in conversation about issues such as air or land pollution within the local community or logging activities in nearby forests. They may also work for organizations focused on global environmental concerns, such as climate change and disappearing rainforests. Activists seek names and contact information for petitions, or encourage on-the-spot membership enrollments or campaign contributions. They also work to persuade people to join the cause themselves by volunteering, writing letters, and voting. With some experience under their belts, activists may help create and lead training workshops for campaigns, offering guidance to beginning activists.

Environmental activists may be involved in the media side of business as well, writing news releases, attending and speaking at news conferences, and developing media contacts to help spread word about the organization's mission, actions, and needs.

An interesting organization for beginning environmental activists is Green Corps (http://www.greencorps.org), which was founded in 1992 with the mission to train environmental organizers. College graduates who are accepted into its year-long program at the Field School for Environmental Organizing receive training from leading figures in the environmental and social change movements, such as Bill McKibben, author and organizer of the "Step It Up" rallies for climate change, and Adam Ruben, political director of MoveOn. org; as well as from groups such as Greenpeace and the Sierra Club. Individuals are sent to help jumpstart campaigns for organizations such as the Rainforest Action Network and Environment America, and must be flexible for possible relocation anywhere across the country during their training period. Trainees are also paid a salary (reported as $23,750 in 2009), and can receive benefits such as paid vacation, sick days, and holidays, as well as student loan repayment plans for those who qualify. Green Corps helps graduates of the program connect to jobs with environmental organizations. Enrollment is extremely competitive, but this is an organization well worth exploring if you are serious about pursuing an environmental activism career.

Seasoned environmental activists may move up to work as environmental activist directors. Responsibilities in this role can range from working closely with marketing and membership departments to strategize and create activist campaigns, to hiring and managing activists. For example, in 2009 Oceana, an ocean conservation group headquartered in Washington, D.C., was seeking an e-activism director to lead its online activism efforts. The director would be responsible for recruiting, retaining, activating, and fundraising for the organization's international base of e-activists. The job also entailed developing and managing Oceana's Web sites, and helping to create an online strategy for e-activism and online giving and organizing.

REQUIREMENTS
High School
Activists rely on a variety of skills and knowledge in their work. A solid educational foundation includes classes in English, communications, biology, environmental studies, social studies, math, foreign language, and computers. Speaking and writing skills are especially important to be an effective activist, so be sure to take classes that also focus on writing and public speaking.

Postsecondary Training
A bachelor's degree is required for some environmental activist positions. Majors can be in anything from communications, journalism, and English, to biology or environmental science. Course work in public policy, political science, community organization, and environmental advocacy is extremely useful in the job. EnviroEducation provides a directory of schools across the country that offer undergraduate and graduate degree programs in environmental studies, with specializations in environmental advocacy or

environmental justice. Search for schools by visiting http://www.enviroeducation.com.

Other Requirements

To do this work well, environmental activists must be passionate and highly knowledgeable about environmental, social, and political issues. They also need to be well versed in the organizations they represent, and able to communicate their passion and knowledge in ways that inspire and motivate people to take action and get involved. Activists work well independently and on teams. Strong, clear communication skills are required. Some activist jobs also require familiarity with e-activism software, online marketing techniques and technologies, and various software programs. A flexible attitude and good sense of humor also help tremendously in dealing with a wide range of people and deadline pressures.

EXPLORING

Learn more about the job by talking to people in the field. The next time you see an environmental activist out on the sidewalk handing out literature and talking to people, stop and see if you can ask them a few questions about the work. Find out what they studied in school and what got them interested in the job. You might be recruited yourself to join in and support the organization, so be prepared for this conversation as well. You can also learn more about the different issues organizations are addressing and the ways activists are getting involved by visiting the Jobs for Change Web site (http://www.change.org).

EMPLOYERS

Many environmental organizations, advocacy groups, and public interest research groups hire environmental activists to help them raise funds and garner support for special projects and campaigns. Activists may work for well-known groups such as Greenpeace and the Sierra Club, or for small organizations and start-ups. Some environmental activists start their own nonprofit environmental groups, to address environmental issues they care deeply about.

STARTING OUT

Jump in and become an environmental activist right now. There's no better way to learn about the job than by actually doing it. Many environmental organizations need volunteers to help them spread the word about their mission and projects, and volunteer work may lead to an entry-level paying position with the organization. You can search for these opportunities by visiting Volunteer Match (http://www.volunteermatch.org) and Idealist.org (http://www.idealist.org). You can also go directly to the Web sites of the organizations that interest you and search for volunteer openings at locations near you. For example, visit The Nature Conservancy's volunteer page at http://www.nature.org/volunteer and use the "search by state" box to find opportunities in your region.

ADVANCEMENT

Environmental activists who start as volunteers can advance to become full-time staff activists. Job titles will vary depending upon the organization. Activists may work as outreach coordinators or campaign coordinators. Some may move up to become campaign workers, assistant campaign directors, and eventually directors. Others may move into other departments within the environmental organization where their communications and outreach skills are needed, such as in membership, public relations, or marketing. Environmental activists can also leave salaried jobs to start their own environmental organizations. Teaching, lecturing, and writing are other avenues for advancement.

EARNINGS

Salaries for environmental activists can vary widely, depending upon level of experience and region. In 2009 a North Carolina-based nonprofit organization in the energy efficiency and renewable energy sector was offering a salary of $40,000 for a full-time community outreach coordinator. The Fund for Public Interest in Denver offered a salary of $23,750 for a full-time citizen outreach director in 2009. A community outreach coordinator working part time for the Fresh Air Fund in 2009 earned $25 per hour. Activists with more years of experience and proven track records in working on successful campaigns for well-known organizations usually command higher salaries.

WORK ENVIRONMENT

Work environments can vary for activists, depending upon the campaign and the type of work they are assigned. Some activists may work strictly in offices, using the computer and telephone for membership and fund-raising campaigns. Others may spend a great deal of time outdoors, assigned to work on certain sidewalks in areas where pedestrian traffic is heaviest. They may be stationed at information booths at conventions, trade shows, school fairs, and even at concerts. Physical stamina and energy are needed to handle the long hours, variable weather conditions, and the demands involved in dealing with the general public. Work hours will vary widely also. Some activists work part-time hours, which can be evenings and weekends. Others work full-time hours but may work in shifts.

OUTLOOK

The forecast for environmental activism looks bright. Demand for advocacy, grant-making, and civic organizations is expected to be on the rise through at least 2016, according to the Department of Labor. More environmental groups exist now than ever before, due to increased concern about clean air and water, conserving natural resources, and protecting habitats and wildlife. Although the job market will be competitive, environmental activists can look forward to decent employment opportunities in the coming years. Those with strong outreach skills, knowledge of e-activism software and tactics, and passion for the environment will fare best in the job market.

FOR MORE INFORMATION

Visit these organizations' Web sites to learn more about environmental advocacy campaigns and projects.

Clean Water Action
http://cleanwateraction.org

Greenpeace
http://www.greenpeace.org

The Nature Conservancy
http://www.nature.org

Oceana
http://na.oceana.org/en

Rainforest Alliance
http://www.rainforestalliance.org

Sierra Club
http://www.sierraclub.org

Get the facts about environmental topics ranging from toxics and waste to compliance and facilities by visiting

Environmental Protection Agency–Envirofacts Data Warehouse
http://www.epa.gov/enviro/index.html

Learn more about the activist training program and find other resources at

Green Corps
44 Winter Street, 4th Floor
Boston, MA 02108-4745
Tel: 617-426-8506
http://www.greencorps.org

Learn more about the issues that advocates, researchers, organizers, and students are studying, and acting on, by visiting

U.S. Public Interest Research Group
44 Winter Street, 4th Floor
Boston, MA 02108-4745
Tel: 617-747-4370
http://www.uspirg.org

Environmental Education Program Directors

OVERVIEW

Environmental education program directors coordinate, manage, and oversee educational programs for students of all ages. They may work for schools, nature centers, museums, parks, and the government. They collaborate with environmental educators to create courses and workshops that teach students about various nature topics, ranging from conservation, biodiversity, wildlife and marine science, ecology, and botany, to environmental policy and regulations, sustainability practices, and other environment-related topics.

HISTORY

The environmental movement in the 1960s and 1970s elevated people's interest in nature, wildlife, the earth, and conservation. 1970 was a pivotal year: It brought the establishment of the Environmental Protection Agency, to standardize and enforce environmental laws and regulations; Earth Day was introduced, to honor the planet; the Clean Air Act was passed; and the Natural Resources Defense Council was created. In the decades since, dialogue about environmental issues has gone global. Numerous books, magazines, documentaries, and television shows have focused on topics such as pollution and hazardous waste, damaged habitats and threatened species. The desire to learn more about the planet in order to better appreciate and safeguard it for future generations has created new and expanded areas of research and education. Many colleges and universities now offer degree programs in environmental studies. And many organizations have created specialty environmental education programs to educate people of all ages about the natural world.

THE JOB

Environmental education program directors create and oversee programs of study that focus on environmental topics, which can relate to animals, plants, land, water, conservation, and natural resources. They work in education departments of museums, conservation and nature centers, parks, zoos, aquariums, or public schools, private schools, colleges, and universities. Their work usually involves hiring and managing educators; researching and creating curriculum for classes, workshops, lectures, and conferences; preparing educational program budgets; and handling other aspects of business if the organization that they work for is small or understaffed. For instance, larger organizations may have dedicated staff to handle everything from enrollment to marketing and promotion. Program directors for small schools or programs may have these tasks added to their job responsibilities.

Most educational program directors have teaching backgrounds. Prior experience in the education field helps them determine the subject matter, the reading and study materials, assignments, and teaching styles that are appropriate for the intended audience, which, for example, will be students if they work for a school, or members if they work for a nonprofit organization. Many directors also have prior work experience as professionals in the field, such as wildlife scientists, biologists, botanists, or green architects, climatologists, or sustainability consultants. Joanne Jarzobski, for example, a science educator at the Cape Cod Montessori School in Massachusetts, has a marine biology background and a passion for whales. Prior to the Montessori school, Joanne worked as education program director for the Provincetown Center for Coastal

(continues on page 50)

INTERVIEW

Joanne Jarzobski, Science/Math Educator and Environmental Education Program Director, Cape Cod Montessori School

Q. How long have you worked for the Cape Cod Montessori School, and what are your job responsibilities?

A. I started working here in September 2008. I am the science teacher, and I also teach math, book group, and do the PR/marketing. I am responsible for developing the science curriculum, which is hands-on, experiential learning using the environment we are in, especially the farm where we are located (Coonamessett Farm, North Falmouth, Massachusetts).

Q. What sparked your interest in this type of work?

A. I have a background in marine biology and directed an at-sea educational program for over 10 years. I originally started working with/studying whales. As a child, my father took me on a whale watch when I was seven and we visited my grandparents on Cape Cod—I was hooked. I wanted to study whales! I'd read and learn as much as I could about them, each year going on a whale watch to see them. Twenty years later I was the one guiding the whale watching trip and helping others meet their dreams of seeing whales.

As my work assisting with humpback whale research and rescue progressed, I realized education was such an important part of it. I always did educational programs at sea on whale watches and this carried over into my developing a love for teaching and wanting to do more of it, directly.

Q. What is your educational and work background?

A. I have my degree in biology, specializing in marine sciences, from Boston University. For the last decade I worked at the Provincetown Center for Coastal Studies (PCCS) and directed their educational programs. My primary responsibilities included directing two different at-sea, environmental education programs for youth of all ages.

I have been responsible for hiring, training, scheduling, and supervising a staff of a dozen marine educators who provide an educational program aboard public whale watching vessels to over 100,000 passengers a year. Through my efforts, the whale watch education program has expended to include a broader range of opportunities, including internships for high school students, lectures to school and civic groups, curriculum packets for classroom teachers, and extended two- to three-day programs focusing on the entire coastal and marine environment of the outer Cape.

In addition, I was responsible for developing, designing, promoting, and fund-raising for MassSail, a public program to promote stewardship and awareness of Massachusetts' marine and coastal environment, as well as the entire ecosystem. Launched in 2005, MassSail programs are conducted entirely in Massachusetts' waters aboard the 125-foot schooner *Spirit of Massachusetts* and include a menu of different programs, which I designed for a broad spectrum of public audiences, age groups, and constituencies. MassSail programs include an intensive two-week, three-college-credit Advanced WhaleSail course, one-week WhaleSail learning adventures for 13–16 year olds, and community day programs from Provincetown to Newburyport, including class-trip day sails, class-trip voyages (three to seven days) and public community programs.

Joanne Jarzobski's commitment to constantly learning, exploring, and sharing has led to special recognition of her contributions to the education field. Honors she has received for her work with people of all ages include: Commonwealth of Massachusetts, Executive Office of Energy and Environmental Affairs, Secretary's Award for Excellence in Environmental Education (2007); Massachusetts Marine Educators "Educator of the Year" (2007); Ruth Hiebert Fellowship for Women in Science (2007); and four Telly Awards for the documentary *Inquiry Into Action* (2003).

(continued from page 47)

Studies, where she managed and directed educational programs that were used for public whale watching trips.

Program directors may also work for education centers that provide educational resources to schools. For example, the Center for Environmental Education (CEE), based at Unity College in Maine (http://www.ceeonline.org), helps schools, nonprofit organizations, and community centers create environmental curriculum that teaches sustainability, climate change, and related issues. CEE helps teachers, students, and community members understand what makes a "green" building green, by using school buildings themselves as objects of study. Students learn if the school's light and heat are derived from renewable sources, and if the school is doing enough recycling and waste reduction or if, and how, it can improve in this area. CEE also creates exhibits and interactive and interpretive panels.

Education program directors may own and run the educational organization as well as manage the educational programs. In addition to creating curriculum, managing teachers, and possibly teaching, program directors may also be responsible for organizing and managing internship and volunteer programs.

REQUIREMENTS
High School
A well-rounded education for environmental education work includes classes in biology, earth science, ecology, social science, history, English, math, computer science, and foreign language. Strong writing and oral communication skills are intrinsic to teaching and managing educational programs. Be sure to also take classes that focus on strengthening your writing and speaking skills.

Postsecondary Training
Environmental education program directors have various degrees depending upon their field of interest. They may have bachelor's and/or masters degrees in biology, marine biology, wildlife science, environmental studies, environmental science, geology, ecology, or botany. Some program directors have combined teaching and environmental studies and science degrees.

Certification or Licensing

Some employers may require education program directors to be licensed educators. Public schools typically require education staff to have bachelor's degrees and teaching licenses issued by state boards of education. Licensure requirements vary by state, but generally require individuals to have undergraduate degrees, to have completed approved teacher training programs, and to have practiced teaching while under supervision by an experienced educator. Private schools do not require licensure.

Other Requirements

Program directors need to be organized, creative, flexible, and patient. They work with a variety of people and personalities every day—students, teachers, administrators and other staff members, as well as parents. The ability to juggle demands while creating stimulating, rewarding educational programs that meet students' needs is important in the work. Strong communication skills are critical, both for writing program outlines and for leading students through different subjects. The work can be demanding, yet program directors need to stay focused. Having an open and curious mind is an asset in the job. Joanne Jarzobski says, "I always knew I wanted to study humpback whales, but I also spent time studying deep sea fish, plankton, water quality, and all things related. [So] never stop learning—be a lifelong learner!" Program directors keep reading and researching throughout their careers. They constantly dig deeper—through books, journals, magazines, films, videos, Web sites, and by attending workshops and classes. This helps them create fresh, up-to-date educational programs, and it also sharpens their brains.

EXPLORING

The best way to start exploring the field is through reading. Joanne Jarzobski says, "Read science magazines and visit Web sites to learn more about what interests you, but also about things you don't know and might find fascinating. Read the newspaper, visit science news Web sites, check out books, and watch documentaries." Some of the magazines and Web sites Joanne regularly checks out, which might interest you also, include *National Geographic*; *Smithsonian*; *Science Daily*; *Science News for Kids* (http://www.sciencenewsforkids. org); *National Geographic Kids* (http://kids.nationalgeographic. com); *NOAA* (National Oceanic and Atmospheric Administration)

Magazine, which is no longer in print but archive issues are posted on its Web site (http://www.magazine.noaa.gov/); and National Aeronautics and Space Administration (http://www.nasa.gov).

Many schools and organizations offer summer environmental education programs for people of all ages. Explore the organizations that interest you most—for example, the World Wildlife Federation (http://www.worldwildlife.org), Sierra Club (http://www.sierra club.org), The Nature Conservancy (http://www.nature.org)—to see what their calendar of events and programs offer. Attend workshops and talks that focus on the environmental issues that intrigue you and that you want to learn more about.

EMPLOYERS

Numerous organizations hire environmental education program directors to run their educational programs. Directors work for schools, community centers, conservation groups, management consulting agencies, museums, and nonprofit organizations. They may also work as independent consultants, running their own businesses and providing educational services to various clients. The U.S. Department of Labor (DoL) does not cite statistics specific to environmental education program directors, but it does show that approximately 443,000 education administrators (who are responsible for setting schools' educational goals and establishing policies and procedures) were employed in the United States in 2006, with the majority working in public or private educational institutions.

The DoL also reports that there were 129,000 instructional coordinators working in the U.S. in 2006. (Coordinators develop curricula, select textbooks and other materials, train teachers, and make sure educational programs meet regulations and standards.) About 40 percent of the coordinators employed in the United States worked in public or private elementary or secondary schools, and 20 percent worked for public or private colleges and universities, and professional schools. The remainder worked for state and local government; individual and family services; child day-care services; scientific research and development services; and management, scientific, and technical consulting services.

STARTING OUT

Environmental education program directors usually start their careers as educators, and prior to that, they start as students.

Learning is a career-long pursuit in this field, so if you are curious and always on the hunt to learn more, this is a profession you will enjoy and succeed in. Many educators also get their start in this career through volunteering at an environmental program at a museum or school. Find one near you and speak with environmental program directors there to learn what they do in their jobs. Ask them how they got started in their careers and what recommendations they may have for ways to explore the field.

ADVANCEMENT

Program directors can advance by working on more complex, specialized projects, and by innovating educational technique and tools. Commitment and dedication to the field, and willingness to share what they have learned, can lead education directors into other areas of education as well, such as writing and creating documentaries and films about the environmental subject in which they have expertise or on topics they are exploring.

EARNINGS

Earnings vary for educational program directors depending upon the employer, the size of the budget, and the region. Salary.com reports that in 2009, education program directors with 10 years of experience had average annual incomes of $100,561, with salaries starting at $69,006 and ranging up to $125,455 or higher. Program directors who work for organizations with small budgets will have lower salaries.

The Bureau of Labor Statistics (BLS) reports that instructional coordinators had average annual incomes of $56,880 in 2008, with salaries ranging from $31,800 to $93,250 or higher. Those who worked for elementary and secondary schools averaged $66,340 per year, while those who worked for the local government earned $52,210. Federally employed instructional coordinators earned higher incomes than those employed in other sectors; their median annual income was $84,360 in 2008.

Education administrators' salaries vary depending on the school level and budget. The BLS reports that education administrators employed in elementary and secondary schools had annual salaries that ranged from $55,580 to $124,250 in 2008. Administrators at postsecondary schools earned between $45,050 to $160,500; and those employed in other industries earned lower salaries, ranging from $38,900 to $124,600.

WORK ENVIRONMENT

Environmental education program directors work 40 or more hours per week. Depending on the programs they direct, hours may be erratic. They work in offices, researching and writing on computers. They also work in classrooms that can be in diverse settings—from office and school buildings, to boats, farms, parks, zoos, or any number of outdoor settings.

OUTLOOK

Job opportunities for environmental education program directors are expected to increase as fast as, or much faster than, the average through 2016. The U.S. Department of Labor reports that the green industry is growing and numerous jobs are expanding to meet demand. While the DoL does not report specifically about environmental education prospects, it does show that employment growth for education administrators is expected to be about as fast as the average for all occupations through 2016. The outlook for instructional coordinators, whose work is also similar to that of environmental program directors, is even better; job growth is expected to be much faster than the average through 2016. Increased interest in environmental issues coupled with new and changing environmental laws and regulations is causing many schools and organizations to create and expand their environmental education programs. Environmental education program directors will be needed to help create and enhance programs to educate youth and adults in various communities.

FOR MORE INFORMATION

Learn more about the Cape Cod Montessori School, its curriculum and projects (including boat building), and the Coonamessett Farm by visiting

Cape Cod Montessori School
PO Box 1381
North Falmouth, MA 02556-1381
Tel: 774-994-7588
http://www.capecodmontessori.org

Find information about green school programs and sustainability education by visiting

Center for Environmental Education
Unity College
90 Quaker Hill Road

Unity, Maine 04988-3712
Tel: 207-948-3131
http://www.ceeonline.org

Find information about marine education by visiting the Web sites of these organizations.

Centers for Ocean Sciences Education Excellence
Office of Marine Programs
University of Rhode Island
Narragansett Bay Campus
Narragansett, RI 02882-1197
Tel: 401-874-6211
Email: cosee@gso.uri.edu
http://www.cosee.net

National Marine Educators Association
703 East Beach Drive
Ocean Springs, MS 39564-5326
Tel: 228-818-8893
Email: nmea@usm.edu
http://www.marine-ed.org

Learn more about education issues, find tools and ideas for educational programs, and check the calendar for upcoming education events by visiting

National Education Association
1201 16th Street, NW
Washington, DC 20036-3290
Tel: 202-833-4000
http://www.nea.org

Find information about membership, certification, conferences, and workshops at

North American Association for Environmental Educators
2000 P Street, NW, Suite 540
Washington, DC 20036-6921
Tel: 202-419-0412
http://www.naaee.org

Environmental Educators

OVERVIEW

Environmental educators teach youth and adults about topics related to the environment. They may work for nonprofit organizations and educate people about green construction or architecture, or how to incorporate sustainability practices into their business operations. Environmental educators may work for conservation centers, educating visitors and members about such things as wildlife habitats, threatened and endangered species, or wetland restoration and preservation projects. They may also educate different age groups in schools and colleges and universities. They use books, journals, films, videos, slides, and other media to educate students and encourage dialogue about environmental topics.

HISTORY

The Environmental Protection Agency (EPA) has been involved in the environmental education field since its inception. Established in 1970 by the White House and Congress to meet growing demand for cleaner water, air, and land, the EPA arrived at a definition of environmental education on which many organizations model their education programs and activities. The purpose of environmental education is to increase "public awareness and knowledge about environmental issues or problems" and to "provide the public with the necessary skills to make informed decisions and take responsible action." Environmental education is a *process*, in which people of all ages and backgrounds are provided with various experiences that give them the skills and capability to make decisions that improve their communities and environments. The EPA emphasizes that environmental education alone is not a solution to environmental problems, for example, on its own, environmental education cannot improve air or water quality. It states on its Web site that a ". . . primary desired outcome of environmental education programs is environmental literacy. . . ." Over time, it equips people with the knowledge, capability, and skills needed to "analyze environmental issues, engage in problem solving, and take action to sustain and improve the environment." And the purpose of the environmental education process is to enable people to weigh various sides of environmental issues so that they can make informed, responsible decisions.

The following are basic components of environmental education:

- Sensitivity to, and awareness, knowledge, and understanding of, the environment and environmental challenges
- Attitudes of concern for the environment and motivation to improve or maintain environmental quality
- Skills to identify and help resolve environmental challenges
- Participation in activities that lead to the resolution of environmental challenges

THE JOB

Environmental educators teach youth and adults of various ages about different aspects of nature. They do not share opinion-based information, but rather provide facts about the environment and help students to think more critically about various environmental issues. Educators may work in the education department of a museum, working with small groups of students in specific age ranges, teaching them about specific exhibits in the museum; or they may offer special workshops and tours to adults, such as nature walks in parks, where they point out and discuss specific flora and fauna. They may be educators for conservation groups, giving lectures to members and the general public about such topics as key identifying factors of wetlands, laws regarding protecting habitats, and what's involved in cleaning up polluted environments.

Environmental educators work on-site at schools, clients' offices, or in their own facilities. Their work involves researching and organizing curricula for classes, lecturing, sharing print and online materials and resources, tracking and recording student attendance, maintaining contact with students throughout classes (in person, and by email and telephone), grading tests and papers, advising students (when needed), meeting with parents to discuss students' progress (depending on student age group), filing reports for school records, and attending educators' conferences and workshops.

Educators are responsible for creating class outlines, which map out the logistics of the classes as well as the specific materials and assignments. Dates, times, locations of classes are laid out. Required reading and research materials are listed—including books, journals, magazines, newspapers, films, Web sites, and other resources. Educators are responsible for clarifying in advance of the class the rules of conduct and basis for grades, which are in accordance with the school or organization. Aspects they address include: what is expected of students, level of participation in classroom settings and in online class chats and forums, specifications for assignments, (deadlines, lengths, style, formatting, reference attribution style, etc.). They may assign group projects and semester-long research papers, and give pop quizzes throughout the duration of the course. Depending on the class level, educators progress students from basic introductions to subjects to more in-depth analysis of topics and subspecialties. Educators present materials in classrooms and lecture halls, in museums, and in outdoor settings. They use a variety of tools and techniques to teach, including blackboards, whiteboards, and computers, as well as group exercises, props, demonstrations, guest speakers, and field trips.

Environmental educators may educate and train other practitioners and the general public in the issues and techniques related to their work. For example, Lauren Yarmouth, principal of New York City-based YRG Sustainability, is an architect who teaches people about green building. She became interested in sustainability while she was studying for her architecture degree. She says, "I was at a very design-focused school when I started to ask the question: What about the functional side of 'form and function'? Why aren't we putting as much emphasis in that as we do in how it all looks? And as I investigated that question further, it unraveled a whole series of additional questions related to resource consumption and design optimization for efficiency, etc. And then I was hooked . . . [It was] as much about wanting to 'do the right thing' as about realizing that we can just be much smarter, much more holistic, and realistic about the decisions we make related to the design, construction, and operations of buildings. And this seemed to me to be much more fun and much more rewarding than any alternative."

An environmental educator with the New York Department of Environmental Conservation holds a copy of an educational magazine called *Conservationist for Kids*. *AP Photo/Mike Groll*

INTERVIEW

Teaching Sustainability: Insights from Lauren Yarmouth, Principal, YRG Sustainability

Q. What kinds of training and workshops do you conduct? And whom do you teach?

A. My classes vary from one-hour sustainability and green-building overviews, to weeklong and semester-long workshops on the technical aspects of making green building happen. I generally teach professionals—CEOs, architects, developers, contractors—on how they can look differently at the work they do to make it more sustainable.

Q. What are the steps involved in teaching?

A. I generally take the approach that we all learn better if we don't feel judged and if we are having fun. . . . So I try to set the stage for dynamic conversations and activities, and really focus on what we *can* do, and how, rather than all the problems with what we are doing. Recently I asked a class to list 20 things that they do in their daily lives that are "not sustainable" and why they do them. Again, I made every effort to let them know that they were not being judged for their responses, including making the answers anonymous in presenting them to the group. But what came out was an amazing series of admissions and realizations that ranged from, "I hire a car service even to go two blocks, just out of habit" to "I leave the AC, TV, and lights on all day sometimes . . . just 'cause." In some cases,

Environmental educators may also work for consulting groups. Companies may hire them when specific issues need to be addressed, such as compliance with environmental laws and regulations, or if they want to educate employees about green business practices. In addition to tasks related to teaching, environmental educators who are independent consultants have a variety of responsibilities related to running their own businesses, such as creating their business identity (including Web sites, stationery, and business cards); marketing and promoting their business; networking to the older students in my class noted that while it was hard for them to recognize their "bad" habits, their kids could point out all the non-green things they were doing really quickly because they are just more aware of these things.

Q. What do you like most about teaching? And what's the most challenging aspect of it?

A. I love it when a student comes up to me after class all lit up and rambles on excitedly about all the things they want to do related to the subject. I love it when I know, can feel, that I am breaking down and communicating an important topic really clearly and well, and I can see the whole class wake up and engage. I love it when months or years after a class, a student will contact me and tell me about how something I did has changed the person they are or the work they do. I love telling stories that make people laugh.

Q. What tips can you share for people who are interested in teaching sustainability?

A. Make it fun and relevant to your audience. Make it personal to you and teach from your own passion (it will show). Use images and stories. Keep it mixed up in terms of format: games, tours, lectures, projects, stories, facts, and more. Ask questions of your students and encourage them to take personal responsibility for their learning. Encourage the individuals in your class to figure out what is meaningful to them in the areas of sustainability and encourage them to focus on that—because they will learn more, [and] better, when they care.

increase business connections; handling the finances, accounting, and filings to comply with IRS laws; hiring and managing staff; and purchasing and maintaining office equipment and supplies.

REQUIREMENTS
High School
Take classes in biology, chemistry, geology, math, history, English, and computer science. If your school offers environmental studies,

agriculture, and/or animal-related classes, take these as well. Knowledge of a foreign language is also useful, particularly for communicating with international students and for overseas education jobs.

Postsecondary Training

An undergraduate degree is required for most environmental education positions. Some employers prefer master's or doctoral degrees in specific topics, coupled with education degrees. Degrees vary depending upon the subject in which environmental educators specialize. Majors may be in biology, botany, ecology, wildlife science, geology, hydrology, meteorology, sustainability practices, environmental architecture, environmental science, environmental studies, environmental planning, to name just a few.

Certification or Licensing

Public elementary and secondary educators must be licensed by the state in which they teach. Requirements vary by state, but in general, all boards of education mandate that teachers have a bachelor's degree, complete an approved teacher training program (meeting the required number of subject and education credits), and complete supervised teaching practice in a classroom. Many states also require teachers to obtain a master's degree in education within a specified number of years after they have begun teaching.

Other Requirements

Communicating ideas in an engaging way and helping students understand topics and explore new ones are the core elements of good teaching. The ability to express yourself clearly, as well as the patience to listen (and listen well) are required to be effective in the job. To say that people skills are also essential is an understatement—people skills are crucial. Interest in sharing thoughts and having dialogue with students of various ages comes with the territory. Environmental educators are passionate and well versed in environmental subjects. They are creative and organized, always coming up with new materials and techniques for educating students. They also continue their own education by reading journals, books, watching films, etc., to stay current on environmental issues and developments.

EXPLORING

Participate in workshops and attend lectures and events at nature centers, parks, and museums near you. You can learn more about the topics being featured, as well as observe the educators' styles of teaching and personally experience what works and what falls flat by audience reaction. Volunteering or interning in an education program department of a nature center or nonprofit organization is also an excellent way to learn more about the job. You can explore volunteer and internship listings by visiting such Web sites as Simply-Hired.com (http://www.simplyhired.com) and Idealist.org (http://www.idealist.org), and keying in the search words "environmental education volunteer" and "environmental education intern."

EMPLOYERS

Environmental educators work for private and public elementary, middle, and secondary schools, as well as for colleges, universities, and professional schools. The Bureau of Labor Statistics reports that there were nearly 2.3 million elementary, middle, and secondary school teachers, and 1.7 million postsecondary teachers employed in the United States in 2006. Environmental educators also work for nonprofit organizations, for-profit companies, government agencies, consulting firms, and educational institutions such as museums and conservation groups.

STARTING OUT

Environmental educators get their foot in the door through internships, volunteer work, or part-time or summer jobs with education departments of museums, parks, conservation groups, or schools. Create a list of the organizations that interest you most and visit their Web sites directly to search for job listings and volunteer and internship programs. Opportunities within these organizations may also exist but may not be widely advertised. Calling the education department or human resources department to find out about current and future employment needs is another step you can take.

Visit the student section of the U.S. Department of Education's Web site (http://www.ed.gov/students/landing.jhtml) to learn more about education careers and for information about colleges, financial aid, grants, and other education-related resources. You can also get an early start in this type of work by reading books about environmental educations. Some good ones to check out include *Earth in Mind: On Education, Environment, and the Human Prospect*, by David W. Orr, and *Beyond Ecophobia: Reclaiming the Heart in Nature Education*, by David Sobel. And don't let these suggestions restrict you; search for other environmental education-related books in your local library, bookstores, and through online booksellers as well.

ADVANCEMENT

Environmental educators who are faculty members of primary or secondary schools may advance to become education administrators, program directors, or department heads. College or university educators who are assistant or associate professors may move up to become full-time, tenured professors and later chairs of departments. Educators may leave salaried positions to start their own businesses, providing consulting services to schools, nonprofit organizations, or corporations. They may also pursue advanced degrees, seek grants or fellowships for research projects, and write papers, articles, or books about environmental topics.

EARNINGS

Salaries for environmental educators vary depending upon employer and the nature of the work. For example, in 2009 Olympic Park Institute in Seattle, Washington, advertised on Indeed.com for a field science educator to lead small groups of students on one- to five-day programs that included hiking and lab studies. The job offered wages of $77 per hour, which meant the annual salary could be $32,032 if the educator led just one eight-hour day program each week for the entire year. Also on Indeed.com, the North Carolina Department of Environment and Natural Resources posted the salary range as $31,622 to $49,290 for an open full-time environmental educator position in 2009.

According to the U.S. Department of Labor, in 2008 annual salaries for public and private elementary school teachers ranged from about $33,400 to $78,030, with median incomes of about $49,330. (Middle school teachers' salaries closely matched: $34,020 to $78,120.) Secondary school teachers had slightly higher incomes in 2008, ranging from $34,280 to $80,970.

Salaries for full-time university professors averaged $73,207, according to the findings of a 2006–2007 survey by the American Association of University Professors. Professors in private independent institutions averaged $84,249 annually.

Educators may supplement their incomes by providing consulting services, teaching courses for other organizations, lecturing, and writing for various publications. Faculty members usually enjoy benefits such as paid holidays and sabbaticals, access to campus facilities, tuition reimbursement or tuition waivers, housing and travel allowances, medical insurance, and retirement plans.

WORK ENVIRONMENT

Environmental educators generally work 40 hours per week. They spend part of their time in offices and libraries, conducting research, creating class materials, grading papers, and responding to emails and phone calls. They also spend time teaching indoors and/or outdoors, depending on the subject matter. They may work indoors in school classrooms and lecture halls, or outdoors in parks, beaches and shoreline areas, and other locations. They may travel to conservation centers to give lectures, or take groups on field trips to learn material firsthand, such as tree-identification walks through forests, or whale-watches in nearby coastal areas.

OUTLOOK

Overall, environmental educators can look forward to decent employment opportunities regardless of the sector in which they work. Job growth for general teachers in private and public schools (including elementary, middle, and secondary) is expected to be about as fast as the average through 2016, according to the U.S. Department of Labor. And postsecondary teachers should have excellent job opportunities through 2016. Employment growth for professors will be much faster than the average due to the expected increase in the 18- to 24-year-old population, resulting in increased college and university enrollment. Also, adults returning to college to enhance their careers and learn new skills will increase demand for educators. More schools and organizations are creating and expanding environmental programs to meet growing interest in this area, and they will be seeking environmental educators who have experience in teaching certain subject areas. Also, due to stricter environmental rules and regulations, many corporations are turning to environmental educators for help in teaching employees and consumers about conservation and sustainability.

FOR MORE INFORMATION

Find job listings, environmental programs for students, and other resources at

North American Association for Environmental Educators
2000 P Street, NW, Suite 540
Washington, DC 20036-6921
Tel: 202-419-0412
http://www.naaee.org

Find educational resources for teaching careers at

U.S. Board of Education
400 Maryland Avenue, SW
Washington, DC 20202-0001
Tel: 800-872-5327
http://www.ed.gov

Visit the Environmental Education section of the EPA's Web site for publications, FAQs about environmental education issues, and to find ideas for environmental projects and campaigns.

U.S. Environmental Protection Agency (EPA)
Environmental Education Division
1200 Pennsylvania Avenue, NW (1704A)
Washington, DC 20460-0001
http://www.epa.gov/enviroed/

Learn more about green building and sustainability by visiting the Web sites of these organizations.

U.S. Green Building Council
2101 L Street, NW, Suite 500
Washington DC 20037-1599
http://www.usgbc.org

YRG Sustainability Consultants
217 Grand Street, Suite 802
New York, NY 10013-4223
Tel: 917-677-8023
Email: info@yrgsustainability.com
http://www.yrgsustainability.com

Fund-raisers, Green Nonprofit Organizations

OVERVIEW

Fund-raisers, also known as *development officers, gift officers,* and *gift coordinators,* strategize advertising campaigns, special events, programs, projects, and products to help green nonprofit companies raise money to accomplish various goals. Fund-raisers work independently and in teams to brainstorm fund-raising plans, identify target markets, determine best times to implement the plans, and decide who to involve in the campaigns, such as staff members, boards of directors, organization members, volunteers, industry experts, and/or celebrities. Fund-raisers create and monitor budgets, hire and manage department staff, write reports and presentations, and also attend—and work during—special fund-raising events such as dinners and concerts.

HISTORY

In the United States the first documented occurrence of fund-raising was in 1643, when Harvard College sent three pastors to

England to cultivate donors, and they succeeded in securing 500 British pounds. Benjamin Franklin was an early philanthropist and fund-raiser who raised money for schools, libraries, relief agencies, and fire departments. Legend has it that Franklin created a system for fund-raising. He suggested making three lists of names, with the first list of names being people you are confident will give money, the second list being people you think will give, and the third being people you doubt will give. You ask the first group for donations. Once you receive them, you show this list of names to the second group, which might convince them that they too should give. And once they give, you show both lists to the third "doubtful" group.

The Scottish American Industrialist Andrew Carnegie amassed great wealth in the late 1800s, and after selling his empire to J.P. Morgan in 1901, spent the rest of his days giving away his fortune to philanthropic interests. He explained his donation philosophy in his essay "The Gospel of Wealth," in which he emphasized the importance of donors' giving away money while they are still alive, to ensure the money is used as intended. Among Carnegie's many donations were the establishment of 3,000 libraries in states throughout the country (with the exception of Alaska and Delaware); millions of dollars to start the Carnegie Institute of Technology in Pittsburgh (now known as Carnegie Mellon University) and the Carnegie Institute in Washington, D.C.; a great deal of financial support to the Tuskegee Institute, which educated African Americans; and funding for 7,000 church organs.

John D. Rockefeller is another well-known capitalist-turned-philanthropist in the early 20th century—he achieved his empire through Standard Oil, a large oil-refining business. He was the first benefactor of scientific medical research, and founded the University of Chicago, the Rockefeller University, the General Education Board, and the Rockefeller Foundation. Rockefeller supposedly gave away $10,000 in shiny new dimes before his death, which is how he received the moniker "the man who gave away shiny new dimes."

Other new developments in the fund-raising profession came about in 1904, when Frank Pierce and Charles Ward, employees of the Young Men's Christian Association (YMCA) created a 27-day fund-raising campaign to raise money for a new YMCA building in Washington, D.C. They created the concept of a "campaign clock" to put pressure on donors to donate before it was too late. They were also the first fund-raisers to hire a publicist and pay for advertising through corporate donations.

Corporate philanthropy developed during World War I, when railroad companies donated money to the YMCA to provide housing to its workers as they traveled across the country. After World War II foundations proliferated, and by 1969 the Tax Reform Act was passed to control this sector. The act prevented individuals from using foundations for their own gain, and mandated foundations to redistribute a percentage of their assets each year. Since the 1960s, the nonprofit sector has expanded to become more professionalized, standardized, and regulated. Many organizations have been created to study, protect, and advance the philanthropy field, such as the Association of Fundraising Professionals, the Independent Sector, and the Association for Research on Nonprofit Organizations and Voluntary Action.

THE JOB

Fund-raisers (development officers) for green nonprofit organizations assist environmental groups in raising money for special projects and programs, and for general help in continuing their causes. The environmental organizations they work for address issues such as conserving and developing natural resources, including land, plant, water and energy resources; clean air and water; and protecting and preserving wildlife and endangered species. Their mission may be to help raise funds for scientific research to address certain environmental issues, or it could be to create educational programs to help raise awareness about specific environmental issues.

Fund-raisers have a variety of responsibilities, including meeting with prospective donors to discuss their interests and goals, regularly meeting and speaking with current donors and addressing their inquiries, hiring and overseeing development staff, organizing and coordinating the details behind fund-raising events and then working throughout the events. Fund-raisers work under a great deal of pressure: The job is goals oriented, with specific donation targets and deadlines set regularly for the short term and long range. To enjoy this type of work, fund-raisers must have thorough knowledge of and passion for the organization's mission.

Fund-raisers develop and maintain relationships with donors. Building rapport and trust with donors is a core element of successful fund-raising. A common misconception is that fund-raising is like sales; in some ways it is, but it is also much more than this. Sales involves a transaction—for instance, if a person needs a product to solve a problem, a salesperson helps the person find it, discusses the benefits and instructs in how to use it, the person buys the product, takes it home, and typically, this ends the relationship (and naturally, this depends on the product). In the nonprofit sector, fund-raising is more commonly defined as "development," and the aim is not so much to "sell" the organization, but rather to develop, or cultivate, long-term relationships with donors. Involving donors in the organization and keeping them involved is essential. Many organizations already have donor bases, which development officers work with while they research ways to expand the base to reach out and secure new donors. Fund-raisers focus on individual giving, corporate giving, and foundation giving.

One example of an environmental group that employs fund-raisers (development officers) is the World Wildlife Federation. In 2009 the organization was seeking to hire a development officer to "identify, cultivate, solicit, and manage the stewardship of foundation donations and prospects, toward achieving its World Wildlife Fund's (WWF) ambitious foundation fund-raising goals." The officer would help manage the writing and reporting process with foundations for select WWF programs; develop and implement fund-raising strategies; and identify new sources to expand the portfolio of foundation supporters. Candidates for the job needed to have an undergraduate degree, at least four years of demonstrated success in writing activities (particularly within the development/fund-raising sector). Knowledge of conservation/environment and/or international development was preferred, and bilingual language skills were a plus.

Many other types of environmental groups—including start-ups and smaller establishments—employ development officers to help them get their messages out and expand their donor bases. Fund-raisers' responsibilities for new and smaller organizations may be more diverse than those of larger organizations. For instance, a junior-level fund-raiser's work may include researching, identifying, and writing grant proposals to foundations; developing and fostering relationships with specific foundation staff (which the organization may even assign to the fund-raiser); assisting in the coordination and launch of new programs; and assisting development staff in administrative tasks such as database entry work and organizing and filing paperwork.

REQUIREMENTS
High School
Fund-raisers are excellent communicators with strong analytical and creative skills. Classes that will give you a solid foundation for

this field include English, communications, speech, math, science (particularly environmental science), history, computer science, and foreign language. Participating in your school's debate team can also help you hone skills in public speaking and persuasion, which will come in handy in fund-raising work.

Postsecondary Training

In 2006 more than 250 colleges and universities offered courses on the management of nonprofit organizations, according to the Department of Labor. About 70 programs offered noncredit courses in fund-raising and nonprofit management, and more than 50 programs offered continuing education courses in nonprofit business. Undergraduate course work in nonprofit business management, fund-raising techniques, environmental science, sustainability, public relations, advertising, marketing, communications, English, finance, statistics, data analysis, computer software programs, and research techniques are beneficial. Although it may not be required for some jobs, familiarity with the organization's subject matter (such as wildlife conservation, wetland restoration, renewable energy) enhances fund-raising success. Fund-raisers who have backgrounds in the areas for which they fund-raise are often able to create campaigns with clear, effective messages that garner good results.

Certification or Licensing

Certification is not required but can enhance a fund-raiser's marketability as well as improve skills and knowledge in fund-raising techniques. CFRE International offers the designation of certified fund raising executive (CFRE) to individuals who meet specific requirements and pass an exam. Recertification is required every three years to maintain the CFRE title.

Other Requirements

Fund-raisers have a strong understanding of what motivates people to donate money and know how to create campaigns that trigger this response. They have analytical skills, which are needed to study results of past campaigns, and are also creative thinkers, a requirement to brainstorm innovative fund-raising tactics. Strong writing skills are also crucial, particularly because some fund-raising positions require grant writing as well. The job is highly pressurized because all fund-raising campaigns set donation goals and time frames. The ability to juggle projects, manage staff, meet budget requirements and deadlines, and stay focused on all of the details throughout is critical to success in this job. Passion for the mission of the organization is also required. What also comes in handy is the ability to keep moving forward and coming up with ideas, even if donation goals fall short. Dedication, persistence, a positive attitude, and energy are useful assets in the fund-raising field. This is hard work. It is not glamorous, and requires mental and physical stamina, and consistent ability to visualize all of the options and strategize the best course of action to take to raise needed funds. Strong knowledge of fund-raising and data management software is also important in the job.

EXPLORING

Learn more about nonprofit development and fund-raising by reading books about the topic. You can find countless offerings at your local library and in bookstores. Two good ones to start with are *Effective Fundraising for Nonprofits: Real-World Strategies that Work*, by Ilona Bray, and *Successful Fundraising: A Complete Handbook for Volunteers and Professionals*, by Joan Flanagan. You can also learn more about the fund-raising field by perusing the Web sites of such groups as the Association of Fundraising Professionals and the Foundation Center (contact information is at the end of this article).

EMPLOYERS

Fund-raisers for green nonprofit organizations work for environment, conservation, and wildlife organizations. They may also work for organizations with missions to advocate for and promote sustainable business and noncommercial operations and practices. According to the Department of Labor, advocacy, grantmaking, and civic organizations had 1.2 million wage and salary jobs in 2006, with many jobs concentrated in California and New York.

STARTING OUT

Fund-raisers get their start in their careers in various ways—some may have gotten their first job in the field through an Internet or newspaper ad, or by applying directly to the company; others may have interned with the organization while in college and started working immediately upon graduation. You can get a head start in this career, while you're in high school, by volunteering or working part time for a nonprofit environmental group near you. Search the Internet to find local organizations with missions that interest you most. You can also find volunteer opportunities through such Web sites as Volunteer Match (http://www.volunteermatch.org) and Idealist.org (http://www.idealist.org/if/as/vol).

ADVANCEMENT

Fund-raisers may start their careers as development assistants or development associates, learning more about the field while in these positions. Within a few years they can move up to become development officers, or gift officers, and later to senior development or senior gift officers. (Titles will vary by organization.) Development directors usually have years of experience and proven track records of fund-raising success. Those who work in full-time positions may advance by starting their own fund-raising consultancies and developing and expanding their client base. They may also mentor and teach students in colleges and universities, as well as lead workshops for professionals who are aiming to expand their skills in and knowledge of the nonprofit sector. Writing books, articles, and blogs about the subject is another path fund-raising professionals may take.

EARNINGS

In 2009 the Association of Fundraising Professionals reported that average annual salaries for fund-raisers in the United States were $61,223. Salary.com shows that in 2009 gift coordinators (a job similar to that of fund-raiser) had annual salaries ranging from $33,114 to $72,694, with median incomes of about $53,103. Major gift officers, who hold senior-level positions in development and fund-raising, had median annual salaries of $71,830 in 2009, with salaries ranging from $48,973 to $91,762 or higher.

WORK ENVIRONMENT

Fund-raisers often work long hours that can stretch into weeknights and weekends. Fund-raising campaigns may last for a day or for weeks at a time. Fund-raising events are often scheduled in the evenings and on weekends, and fund-raisers are usually on hand to oversee that all goes according to plan. They may spend some time traveling to meet with clients, view prospective sites for events, and attend conferences and workshops. They mainly work in offices, but may also spend some time outdoors if they work for environmental groups that host fund-raising events and programs in natural settings.

OUTLOOK

In 2009 fund-raising was ranked among *U.S. News and World Report*'s "Top 30 Careers." Fund-raising was given an A in all categories, including job market outlook, prestige, and job satisfaction. Fund-raisers for green nonprofit organizations can expect good employment opportunities in the years to come. Increased demand for advocacy, grantmaking, and civic organizations services are expected to contribute to job growth in the nonprofit sector, according to the *Occupational Outlook Handbook*. Fund-raisers will be needed to help emerging as well as longstanding environmental groups develop and maintain relationships with donors, and increase funds to help them continue to address their missions.

FOR MORE INFORMATION

Find membership information and upcoming conferences and events at
Association of Fundraising Professionals
4300 Wilson Boulevard, Suite 300
Arlington, VA 22203-4168
Tel: 800-666-3863
http://www.afpnet.org

Learn more about certification in fund-raising by contacting
CFRE International
4900 Seminary Road, Suite 670
Alexandria, VA 22311-1811
Tel: 703-820-5555
Email: info@cfre.org
http://www.cfre.org

Find information about grant writing and other resources at
The Foundation Center
79 Fifth Avenue, 16th Street
New York, NY 10003-3076
Tel: 212-620-4230
http://foundationcenter.org

Grant Writers, Green Nonprofit Organizations

QUICK FACTS

School Subjects
Communications
English

Personal Skills
Analytical/creative
Educating/writing

Work Environment
Indoors
One location

Minimum Education Level
Bachelor's degree

Salary Range
$25,844 to $53,883 to
$61,228+

Certification or Licensing
Voluntary

Outlook
About as fast as the average

OVERVIEW

Grant writers help nonprofit companies secure funding for operational expenses and special projects and programs so that they can fulfill their missions. They identify prospective donors, research and write grant applications and requests, monitor and follow-up on requests, and maintain records of grants and grant requests. They collaborate with other grant writers, development managers, and association employees in their work.

HISTORY

The United States has a long history of creating and running public-serving and member-serving organizations to address issues. Early settlers created charitable and other voluntary associations such as hospitals, orphanages, fire departments, and churches to address needs, and ills, within society. Alexis de Tocqueville, an Aristocratic Frenchman who authored the book *Democracy in America*, visited the United States in 1831 and noted, "Americans of all ages, conditions, and dispositions constantly unite together. Not only do they have commercial and industrial associations to which they all belong but also a thousand other kinds, religious, moral, serious, futile. . . . Americans group together to hold fetes, found seminaries, build inns, construct churches, distribute books. . . . They establish prisons, schools by the same method. . . . I have frequently admired the endless skill with which inhabitants of the United States manage to set a common aim to the efforts of a great number of men and to persuade them to pursue it voluntarily." Many of these early organizations that de Tocqueville mentioned were able to fill social welfare program gaps that the state and federal governments could not address—a situation that holds true to a certain degree today.

In the centuries since de Tocqueville's visit, Americans are still banding together over certain causes. The nonprofit sector has, as a result, expanded to include a variety of charitable organizations and foundations with diverse missions that address the needs of people, animals, and the planet. Private foundations developed in the early 20th century, thanks to philanthropic interests of wealthy individuals such as Andrew Carnegie and John D. Rockefeller, and continue today to make significant contributions in the grant-making sector. After World War II, corporate philanthropy developed, further growing the nonprofit sector and offering another area from which to seek funding for crucial projects and programs within communities. The field of grant writing has similarly expanded and advanced over time, with the grant request process now more formalized and standardized than in previous years, and grant writers receiving more recognition for their skills and contributions in the nonprofit sector.

THE JOB

A grant is specific funding that donors—such as the U.S. government, private foundations, or public corporations—give to organizations and individuals to use for specific projects and needs. Grants require no repayment and are given to recipients that have submitted required grant application paperwork, accompanying forms, and specific details about the project or program that requires funding, all of which is known as a *grant proposal.* Grants can be given to nonprofit companies, charitable organizations, educational facilities, or individuals.

Grant writers help nonprofit organizations secure funding for special projects and programs, and for operational costs such as general overhead and payroll. Companies may need funding for any number of things. In nonprofit environmental organizations, the needs may range from funding to help create company literature such as brochures and business cards, to kayaks and paddles to help kids explore certain waterways in their community.

Grant writers first need to have a thorough understanding and knowledge of the environmental organization for which they are writing the grant request. They need to know its mission, its programs, its staff, and its history. If they are freelance writing for the client, this is the first phase of research. They then research prospective donors, learning about their donation history and current and future programming plans, to determine if the purpose of the grant lines up with the donor's mission and interests. Grant writers keep up with project planning and organizational finances so they can make recommendations for grants to pursue. They write the grant proposals and liaise with grant makers to address questions and furnish further information as needed. They also write progress reports regarding grant requests.

An important element of a grant writer's job is getting the organization's "voice" right for the writing. Each organization has a style and tone of communication, which can be found consistently throughout all of its past and current communication pieces—including annual reports, brochures, promotional materials, newsletters, and other publications—as well as on its Web site. This is more than how the company treats the spelling of certain words (for instance, a British organization will spell the word as organisation), although this is extremely important to pay attention to as well. The company's communication style may be more corporate and factual, or more laid-back and conversational. It may prefer long sentences or extremely short sentences. Grant writers are careful to model their writing on the organization's style, and refrain from introducing their own voices and styles into the pieces.

Grant writing revolves around requests for funding, so the ability to persuade through words is tantamount. Grant application writing may be free form, or funders may have specific grant application forms. Most grant makers have guidelines that grant writers adhere to. The application process can sometimes be complicated, with applications requiring various and multiple attachments such as financial statements and legal documents. The ability to organize a variety of materials—from interviews with people to data from charts, tables, and graphs—is critical in the job. It often requires translating sometimes complex material into language readers will understand. For some positions, knowledge of biology, environmental science, ecology, and environmental laws and regulations may be required. Successful grant writers are able to convey to prospective donors why the grant is essential by substantiating the request with descriptions of the organization's past accomplishments in environmental program areas, statistics regarding the problems that are occurring in the environment and communities because of the lack of attention to and funding for specific areas, and specific plans for how the money will be used and what the short-term and long-term goals are if the money is awarded.

Donors award grants for many reasons, but mostly because the organization requesting the grant has a solid reputation in the field; the program for which it is seeking funding is important and crucially needed; the request lines up with an area in which the donor plans to focus; and the writing is engaging, convincing, and technically accurate. Many organizations prefer to hire grant writers who have proven track records—meaning, a high percentage of grants have been awarded because of their proposals. This is not to say that beginning grant writers will not be able to find work; but it does mean that newcomers to the field will need to be especially careful and precise with grammar, spelling, and punctuation, and be able to show a thorough understanding of the organization's background and mission.

REQUIREMENTS
High School
Strong research and writing skills are the foundation for grant writing work. Hone your skills through English and communication classes. Also be sure to balance your studies with classes in history, science, math, foreign language, and computer science. Environmental and physical science classes will be especially useful for some environmental grant writing jobs. If your school offers any classes or workshops in research skills, take these as well.

Postsecondary Training
An undergraduate degree coupled with several years of experience is usually required by companies seeking to hire grant writers. Majors may be in English, journalism, communications, or other areas related to the mission of the organizations seeking fund-raising assistance, such as biology, wildlife science, wetland science, etc. College classes that are helpful in this career include English, communication, math, nonprofit business management, advertising, public relations, social sciences, environmental studies, computer software programs, statistics, data analysis, and research techniques. Some organizations may require advanced degrees.

In 2006 more than 250 colleges and universities offered courses on the management of nonprofit organizations, according to the Department of Labor. About 70 programs offered noncredit courses in fund-raising and nonprofit management, and more than 50 programs offered continuing education courses in nonprofit business.

Certification or Licensing
Certification is voluntary. Because there are no degree programs specific to grant writing, certification might enhance a grant writer's chances of securing work. The American Association of Grant Professionals offers certification through its Grant Professionals Certification Institute. (Find more information at the end of this article.)

Other Requirements
Grant writers have excellent verbal and written communication skills, are organized and detail oriented, and work well independently and on teams. The work entails researching and understanding the organization for which they are writing grant proposals, as well as understanding the prospective funder's company. The ability to speak with a variety of people and listen closely to what they have to say is essential. Interviewing employees, consultants, and specialists with various backgrounds is a large part of the job. Quick learners who can work well under pressure to meet deadlines do well in this type of work. Knowledge of budgeting and financial aspects of grant applications is also important. Naturally, not all grants are awarded, and grant writers must be able to deal with disappointment when this happens and move on.

EXPLORING
There is plenty of information in print and online about the grant writing process. Some books that can help you learn more about the field include *Getting Funded: The Complete Guide to Writing Grant Proposals*, by Mary Hall and Susan Howlett; *Demystifying Grant Seeking: What You Really Need to Do to Get Grants*, by Larissa Golden Brown and Martin John Brown; and *Writing for a Good Cause*, by Joseph Barbato and Danielle Furlitch. You can also try your hand at grant writing by practicing on your own. For guidance, check out the Minnesota Council on Foundations' online guide for "Writing a Successful Grant Proposal" (http://www.mcf.org/mcf/grant/writing.htm). It will walk you through what funders seek in grant requests, how to best organize your material, types of words and phrases to use, and an FAQ list. You can also look at real grants that have succeeded in the past by visiting the "Sample Proposals"

page on the SchoolGrants' Web site (http://www.k12grants.org/samples).

EMPLOYERS

Grant writers work for a variety of nonprofit organizations—from environmental groups to hospitals and schools. According to the Department of Labor, advocacy, grantmaking, and civic organizations had 1.2 million wage and salary jobs in 2006. These types of organizations are located throughout the United States, but the greatest numbers of jobs are found in California and New York. Most establishments in this industry are small, with nine out of 10 organizations employing fewer than 20 employees. Many jobs are in establishments that employ fewer than five people. Many grant writers also find their jobs through volunteer work, and some also work in part-time grant writing positions while also running their own businesses.

STARTING OUT

Grant writers get started in their careers in any number of ways—they may have previous experience in nonprofit organizations in grant writing, development, membership, or other areas. They may be journalists, writers, editors, or even educators who have a strong interest in the mission of their grant writing client or employer. They also may be specialists in the field the organization represents, such as scientists, doctors, or engineers, and have knowledge and experience in the subject matter. A great way to gain early experience in this type of work is by helping out a local nonprofit environmental group in your community. If a particular one comes to mind that interests you, contact them to see if they have any programs in the works that can use some start-up funding or additional donor support. Volunteer to write a grant proposal or two, and follow the guidelines suggested in the "Exploring" section. You can also find environmental groups that you can volunteer your grant writing help to by searching the nonprofit organization list at Volunteer Match (http://www.volunteermatch.org).

ADVANCEMENT

Advancement for grant writers depends upon the structure of the organizations they work for. With years of experience and success in securing grants, grant writers may move up to senior grant writing positions, and can later advance to become directors of development. They may expand their education by securing advanced degrees, and hone their skills through professional certification. Experienced grant writers may also leave salaried positions to start their own grant writing businesses, and expand their services to help organizations in other specialty areas. Another form of advancement may be in sharing knowledge and mentoring students, through teaching and writing books and articles about the experience and practice of grant writing.

EARNINGS

Salary.com reports that salaries for grant writers ranged between $41,792 to $68,827 in 2009, with median incomes averaging about $53,883. Grant writers with less than one year of experience earned $25,844 to $37,232 annually, and those with five to nine years of experience had salaries ranging from $39,873 to $56,563, according to Payscale.com statistics. Those with more experience and proven track records of securing grants for reputable organizations and well-known, successful programs are usually able to secure salaries of $61,228 or more. In addition to salaries, benefits for full-time grant writers can include health and dental insurance; paid holidays, vacations, and medical leave; disability benefits; and profit sharing.

WORK ENVIRONMENT

Grant writers usually work 40-hour workweeks in offices. Hours may be longer if deadlines are approaching for certain grant applications. They may travel to conduct interviews for grant proposals; for instance, to learn more about specific projects and programs, and gain a better understanding of the organization's mission and goals. They may include quotes from interviewees to emphasize and bolster the importance of the funding for the grant. Freelance grant writers may work anywhere—home offices, clients' offices, public or school libraries, etc.

OUTLOOK

The U.S. Department of Labor (DoL) forecasts average employment growth for all writers and editors through 2016. Growth of jobs in the nonprofit sector will be attributed to increased demand for advocacy, grantmaking, and civic organization services. For instance, the elderly population is growing, which should result in heightened need for services catering to the needs of the elderly, such as home health care. Increased cultural diversity in the United States is also giving rise to more nonprofits that are dedicated to ethnic and cultural needs. Environmental organizations are also on the rise due to increased awareness about environmental issues and stricter laws and regulations. According to the DoL, although state and local governments are often expected to help fund social service roles, many governments may lack the resources to meet the growing need. Advocacy, grantmaking, and civic organizations will be more heavily relied upon to offer expertise in this arena. Governments will also be contracting consultants for some services, which will continue to be a major source of employment growth in the advocacy, grantmaking, and civic organizations industries. Grant writers are expected to have decent job opportunities in the years to come, but can also expect competition to be keen, particularly in environmental organizations, as many people are attracted to this sector. Those with solid academic and work backgrounds, excellent writing and research skills, and proven success in grant writing will have better chances of securing work.

FOR MORE INFORMATION

Learn more about certification and find other resources for grant writing by visiting

American Association of Grant Professionals
1333 Meadowlark Lane, Suite 105
Kansas City, KS 66102-1200
Tel: 913-788-3000
Email: info@grantprofessionals.org
http://grantprofessionals.org

Visit the Web sites of these associations to learn more about membership and find upcoming conferences and events.

Association of Fundraising Professionals
4300 Wilson Boulevard, Suite 300
Arlington, VA 22203-4168
Tel: 800-666-3863
http://www.afpnet.org

Association for Research on Nonprofit Organizations and Voluntary Action
550 West North Street, Suite 301
Indianapolis, IN 46202-3491

Tel: 317-684-2120
http://www.arnova.org

Find information about grant writing and other resources at
The Foundation Center
79 Fifth Avenue, 16th Street
New York, NY 10003-3076
Tel: 212-620-4230
http://foundationcenter.org

Find nonprofit news, publications, conferences, forums, and other resources at
Independent Sector
1602 L Street, NW, Suite 900
Washington, DC 20036-5682
Tel: 202-467-6100
Email: info@independentsector.org
http://www.independentsector.org

Green Reporters

QUICK FACTS

School Subjects
English
Math
Science

Personal Skills
Communication/ideas
Research/writing

Work Environment
Indoors, occasionally
outdoors
One location

Minimum Education Level
Bachelor's degree

Salary Range
$20,180 to $34,850 to
$156,200+

Certification or Licensing
Not required

Outlook
Little or no change

OVERVIEW

Green reporters cover a broad range of science- and environment-related topics to inform the public about environmental developments and issues. Reporters may also specialize in covering one specific environmental issue. Reporting entails reading and researching subject matter; identifying sources for interviews; creating interview questions and conducting interviews; gathering material and writing and editing articles for print and online newspapers, magazines, and journals for environmental and scientific consulting and educational groups, and public relations firms.

HISTORY

Environmental journalism has roots in nature writing. In the 1800s Ralph Waldo Emerson and Henry David Thoreau were known for their essays and lectures about nature and philosophy. At the turn of the 20th century, books and poems by John Muir and John Burroughs introduced people to such topics as the mountains of California and the preservation of land and wilderness. Ecologist Aldo Leopold continued enlightening the general public about environmental ethics and wildlife management in his writings in the 1930s and 1940s.

Environmental journalism became entrenched in popular media starting in the 1960s and 1970s. Kicked off by the book *Silent Spring* in 1962 about pesticides harming birds and the environment, and the passage of the Wilderness Act in 1964, numerous environmental and wildlife laws followed, and grassroots environmental organizations were established throughout the country to tackle environmental issues such as endangered species and air and water pollution. More people were learning about environmental issues due to conservation organizations' direct mail campaigns and brochures, and through mass media coverage. The 1980s bought a whole new set of problems and simultaneously created another area for reporters to cover: environmental disasters. Breaking news throughout the decade featured stories about such crises as the Bhopal gas tragedy in India, the Chernobyl nuclear disaster in the Ukraine, and the Exxon Valdez oil spill in the United States. Green reporters continue to report on various environmental issues—from mercury in fish to greenhouse gases in the atmosphere—to educate and inform the general public and to call attention to situations and subjects that may need further investigation to remediate problems and ensure environmental health.

THE JOB

Green reporters, also known as *environment reporters*, cover science- and environment-related subject matter. Topics they report on may include air pollution, water concerns, waste management issues, brownfields, local environmental issues, biodiversity, global climate change, ozone depletion, forests, habitat concerns, wildlife, sustainable development, environmental education, occupational health, environmental disasters, and the list goes on. They may specialize in one or two areas, or work as general environmental reporters. They cull stories from any number of sources, such as press releases and press conferences, current events, blogs, e-newsletters, conversations that trigger ideas, or editors who assign them stories to cover.

Reporters' duties vary depending on their years of experience in the field. Those with more experience usually handle more complex assignments. In general, however, core responsibilities that most reporters have include writing articles, stories, and broadcast materials. (Broadcast reporters travel to the sites of stories and provide live coverage of events.) Preparing and conducting interviews is a big part of the job and lays the groundwork for each story. After the interviews are over, reporters conduct research and investigations to ensure the information is accurate. They also do this to verify that all data they have collected is accurate before submitting pieces for publication. If any quotes are unclear, they contact interviewees to clarify or rephrase information. They reference reports and journals, statistics and findings from surveys, and analyze and gather information that is pertinent, interesting (or startling), and gives their story a twist or bolsters the ideas it presents to readers. Reporters also attend and tape press conferences and speeches, and transcribe recordings using transcription software programs or other media.

Environment reporters may also work as bloggers for Web sites of publications. The magazine *Mother Jones* described an available environmental reporter/blogger position as follows: ". . . You will write for both the magazine and the website, a mix of long-form investigation and fast-paced, incremental reporting and blogging. Position is based in one of our two editorial offices (though applicants with a strong existing audience who live elsewhere will be considered) and will involve travel. Applicants should have at least three years of reporting experience and an affinity for both nitty-gritty policy/political coverage and compelling, scene-based reporting."

Self-employed green reporters also need to maintain their current client base while networking to attract new clients and assignments. Juggling current work with marketing and promotion efforts is challenging and time-consuming, but necessary to maintain contacts and keep projects circulating. Independent reporters are also responsible for handling their business accounting and tax filings, creating and maintaining their own Web site, and keeping up with news and developments in the field by attending conferences and participating in educational programs.

REQUIREMENTS
High School
Reporting and writing skills are essential, as is an understanding of environmental issues and scientific topics. Classes that will help you in this career include environmental studies, biology, chemistry, geology, math, social studies, economics, psychology, English, writing, and computer science. Foreign language classes are beneficial also. Be sure to participate in your school's newspaper and any writing clubs.

Journalists crowd around the River Simple hydrogen car as it is launched in London in June 2009. *Getty Images*

Postsecondary Training

An undergraduate degree is required in this field. Many green reporters have bachelor's degrees in journalism, mass communications, English, or in science specialties, such as environmental or wildlife science. Degrees may also be in economics, business, or political science.

According to the Bureau of Labor Statistics, more than 1,500 educational institutions offer journalism, communications, and related programs. Of these, 109 were accredited by the Accrediting Council on Education in Journalism and Mass Communications in 2007. Course work generally focuses on liberal arts and journalism, and can include such subjects as mass media, basic reporting and copyediting, history of journalism, and press law and ethics. Broadcast students take classes in radio, TV news, and production. Newspaper or magazine writing students usually specialize in news-editorial journalism. They take computer software classes in order to learn how to combine online story text with video and audio elements and graphics.

Schools that offer master's or Ph.D. degree programs in journalism may prepare students specifically for news careers; or they may prepare journalism teachers, researchers and theorists, and advertising and public relations workers.

Other Requirements

Green reporters must have a solid grasp of environmental, political, economic issues and factors to write intelligent, factually based stories. Intuition about what is, and isn't, news is also essential to success in the job. Good reporters are good listeners who pay close attention to details and always ask questions when something is not immediately clear to them. They have strong research and analytical skills, and are skilled in gathering a variety of data and information to create educational and thought-provoking articles. Clear, concise writing and skill in translating complex material to layperson language is intrinsic to the job. They understand their readers well and know how to write in ways that will engage them. Green reporters also need to have strong computer graphics and desktop publishing skills, as well as knowledge of Internet-based technology and other multimedia. Photography skills may also be required for some positions.

EXPLORING

Read print and online publications to stay up to date on news about the environment and scientific trends and discoveries. Visit the Web sites of conservation groups to see what projects are developing and learn more about the environmental problems certain regions are facing and solutions they may be devising. Magazines such as *Popular Science* and *Scientific American* will also help you stay in the scientific loop. You can also find a comprehensive list of organizations for journalists at Reporter.org (http://www.reporter.org)—they're hyperlinked so all you need to do is click and explore.

EMPLOYERS

Environment reporters work for newspapers and periodicals, scientific journals, and for educational and environmental organizations. The Bureau of Labor Statistics reports that there were 67,000 news analysts, reporters, and correspondents employed in the United States in 2006. More than half worked for newspaper, periodical, book, and directory publishers. About 23 percent worked in radio and television broadcasting, and 11 percent worked as freelancers or stringers.

STARTING OUT

Many green reporters get their start by working on their high school and college papers, as well as through internships with publishers.

Get onto your school paper and start researching and writing about the science topics that are on everyone's minds. Ask your science teachers for suggestions for topics. Read newspapers to see what environment reporters are writing about. Professional associations for reporters also offer useful resources, such as the Society of Environmental Journalists and the American Society of News Editors (ASNE). Interning is also an excellent way to explore the job while honing skills you can use in future work. ASNE lists internships under the resources section of its Web site. (Contact information is located at the end of this article.)

ADVANCEMENT

Many environment reporters start out as general-assignment reporters or sometimes as freelance reporters (stringers). General-assignment means they report on general topics such as civic and club meetings, court proceedings, speeches, and they may also write obituaries. With some experience they can advance to more difficult assignments and specialize in a field, such as the environment. Environment reporters are usually already seasoned professionals in the field. If they work for larger publications, they may advance to senior writer or managing editor positions. Reporters who work for small publications can move up by taking positions at larger publications. Reporters with enough experience and stature in the field can become columnists, correspondents, announcers, or public relations specialists. Some may move into broadcast journalism, and move up to become program managers, supervising other reporters. They may also write books and teach in colleges and universities.

EARNINGS

Salaries for new reporters, correspondents, and analysts vary depending upon the medium in which they work. For example, broadcast journalists usually earn higher salaries than newspaper reporters. In 2008 news reporters and correspondents had median annual incomes of $34,850, with the lowest paid 10 percent averaging $20,180 and the top paid 10 percent earning $77,480 or more annually, according to the Department of Labor. The top paying states were District of Columbia, New York, Maryland, Rhode Island, and New Jersey. Broadcast news analysts had higher incomes than news reporters and correspondents in 2008, ranging from $23,470 to $156,200.

WORK ENVIRONMENT

Green reporters work long hours indoors, conducting online research, phone interviews, and responding to emails. They also travel to sites to study environments, take notes, and conduct in-person interviews. Travel can vary widely; reporters may be in a laboratory one day, interviewing scientists and researchers, and outside by a polluted coastline the next, speaking with environmental scientists and marine biologists. Physical fitness comes in handy when covering outdoor terrain, and a flexible attitude is needed to effectively adjust to changes that regularly crop up during the course of the workday.

OUTLOOK

The Department of Labor predicts that employment of general news analysts, reporters, and correspondents will show little or no change through 2016. Publishing and broadcasting industries continue to consolidate and improve, reducing the need for reporters. Some job openings are expected to occur due to the need to replace people who retire or leave positions for other jobs. On the positive side, however, the DoL states that "Talented writers who can handle highly specialized scientific or technical subjects will have an advantage."

Online newspapers and magazines, and small local papers and news stations will offer more employment opportunities for reporters. The DoL also predicts that beginning newspaper reporters will have better odds of finding more freelance opportunities than staff positions in the coming years. Students with degrees in journalism as well as in another subject, such as politics, economics, or biology, will have an advantage over those without additional background knowledge. Competition will still be keen for green reporter positions at newspapers and magazines. Strong clips and a grasp of environmental issues, coupled with an excellent academic background, can give reporters an edge in the job hunt.

FOR MORE INFORMATION

Find membership information and business basics for journalists and authors at

American Society of Journalists and Authors
1501 Broadway, Suite 302
New York, NY 10036-5505
Tel: 212-997-0947
http://www.asja.org

Find internships, job listings, training programs and seminars at
American Society of News Editors
11690B Sunrise Valley Drive
Reston, VA 20191-1436
Tel: 703-453-1122
http://asne.org

Learn more about environment, energy, science, health, and climate reporting at
Society of Environmental Journalists
PO Box 2492
Jenkintown, PA 19046-8492
Tel: 215-884-8174
Email: sej@sej.org
http://www.sej.org

Inbound Tour Guides

QUICK FACTS

School Subjects
Geography
History
Speech

Personal Skills
Helping/teaching
Leadership/management

Work Environment
Indoors and outdoors
Primarily multiple locations

Minimum Education Level
High school diploma

Salary Range
$15,000 to $45,000 to
$61,000+

Certification or Licensing
Required for some positions

Outlook
Much faster than the average

OVERVIEW

Tour guides lead groups of people to sites of interest. Guides who lead short excursions to famous American destinations are called *inbound tour guides*. Inbound tours may last a few hours or overnight. Guides provide an important service to the travel and tourism industry by promoting certain areas of the country and introducing people to interesting and innovative communities, structures, and ideas. There were 40,000 tour guides employed in the United States in 2006.

HISTORY

The United States is viewed by many as a land of wealth, excitement, and glamour—in short, a dream destination. Many cities and attractions have built a reputation as travel musts, among them Las Vegas, Hollywood, New York City, Disneyland, and Disney World. New York City alone attracts 47 million foreign and American tourists each year. So many people travel to U.S. cities that a tourism subspecialty has evolved—inbound tour guides. Inbound tour guides lead tours for foreign visitors as well as Americans who are on vacation. Also, a recent development in the inbound tour field is ecotours—excursions to environmentally friendly destinations such as parks, public gardens, aquariums, green-certified hotels and restaurants, and to cities that are becoming renowned for their efforts to operate more sustainably.

THE JOB

Inbound tour guides take passengers on short excursions that may last a few hours, a full day, or even overnight. A recent attraction in the field is inbound ecotours. In the past, ecotour companies focused mostly on leading tours *outward*, to faraway exotic, fragile areas such as the Galapagos Islands in Ecuador and the Tapanti National Park in Costa Rica. These areas are still a main draw, but with interest in environmental issues taking deeper root nationally, many tour companies now also offer day or overnight ecotours that can be done by foot (as in hiking), by bike, or even by horseback. These tours focus on introducing people to areas in the United States they may not know much about, and educating them about such things as conservation, ecology, and geology.

There are many tour groups offering day trips to natural regions throughout the United States. EcoTours of Oregon, for example, introduces people to Oregon's remaining virgin forests and other natural areas through day hikes to Mount Hood, Mount St. Helens, and other destinations in Oregon and Southwest Washington. On the other side of the country, New York City-based Hines Tours Inc. leads day tours through natural areas in the New York region, including the Catskill, Pocono, and Berkshire Mountains, and the Delaware Water Gap. Hines Tours' philosophy is one that many ecotour companies no doubt embrace: "We are committed to protecting our region's natural resources and improving outdoor recreation opportunities for everyone, especially for New Yorkers who are unaware of the many amazing beautiful natural areas within just hours of drive from NYC. We believe this is best achieved through education and providing a hands-on experience for everyone. We do our best and go far in our research to find remarkable natural tour destinations/activities for you to enjoy. We believe that our regions' scenic areas . . . sensitive ecosystems and wildlife habitats . . . should be respected and protected forever for generations to come."

Another type of ecotour might be a tour that focuses on sustainable living. For instance, the City of Portland's Bureau of Planning and Sustainability offered a tour of green homes in 2009; it was called "Build it Green!" The tour featured multiunit as well as single-family homes and buildings that were either already built or in the process of being constructed in communities throughout Portland, Oregon. In the tour, people could learn more about the features that comprise more sustainable living, such as resourced and recycled building materials, ecoroofs, energy conservation tactics like rainwater harvesting and radiant or hydronic heating. Tour guides helped people appreciate and understand these details.

Inbound tour guides are responsible for making all of the necessary arrangements for a trip before departure, such as booking transportation, which can be buses, trains, vans, or airline flights; lodge or hotel rooms; and tables at restaurants. They may even cater tours with boxed lunches and dinners. If anyone in the tour group has special requirements, such as dietary requirements or wheelchair accessibility, the guide must attend to these needs in advance. Recreational guides are also responsible for equipment, making sure people are outfitted appropriately and if equipment is being rented to people, that it functions properly and is returned in good condition and accounted for at the end of the trip.

Guides may also be involved in the communications end of the business—researching and writing descriptions of the places that will be visited—for the tour company's Web site, and promotional brochures and flyers. Depending on the size and structure of the tour company, they may also respond to email and phone queries, handle booking trips and financial transactions, and send out trip confirmations and schedule updates.

Guides also plan the group's entertainment and make any necessary advance reservations to plays, sporting events, or concerts. They may also contact other guides with specialized knowledge to give group tours of various locations. For example, for a group visiting Chicago, the tour manager might arrange for a guided tour of the Art Institute one day and a tour of famous city landmarks and architecture on another day.

Inbound tour guides must make sure that everything goes as planned, from transportation and accommodations to entertainment. Inbound guides should be familiar with the locations they are visiting and be able to answer questions and provide educational and entertaining commentary throughout the trip. They make sure that all members of the group stay together, taking population counts every so often, so that the group remains on time for various arrivals and departures.

An inbound tour guide points to an attraction as she leads a group of tourists through a mountain range. *Wolfgang Amri/Shutterstock Images*

REQUIREMENTS

High School

If you hope to become a tour guide, there are several high school courses you can take that will prepare you for the position and improve your chances of finding a job. Perhaps the single most valuable class is a foreign language. Tour guides who can speak a second language fluently will be in the greatest demand.

A good tour guide should have a grasp of his or her destination's history and culture; therefore, classes in social studies, sociology, geography, environmental studies and science, geology, and history are excellent choices. Courses in art history or appreciation are also helpful. Much of the tour guide's work is in communicating with people, and may often involve speaking to groups of travelers— classes in speech can help prepare you for this job. Gym classes and sports are also important for future recreational guide work.

Postsecondary Training

Although there is no formal education requirement for becoming a tour guide, many guides do have some postsecondary training.

Many two- and four-year colleges, as well as trade and professional schools, offer courses in tour management and guiding. Some large travel agencies offer their employees in-house training classes.

Some tour guides, especially those interested in leading special interest tours such as ecotours, have bachelor's or master's degrees in various subjects, such as environmental science, wildlife science, ecology, botany, or geology. If you hope to combine your interest in a particular field with a career as a tour guide, you should focus heavily on your area of interest, as well as taking supplemental classes in public speaking and travel and tourism, where available.

Certification or Licensing

Many outdoor guides are licensed by their state's department of conservation. For example, the New York State Forest Rangers regulates the licensing of outdoor guides in New York State. New York guides must be at least 18 years old and offer services for hire that include directing, instructing, or aiding other people in hiking; rock or ice climbing; whitewater rafting, canoeing, and/or kayaking; fishing; hunting; or camping. To be licensed, guides must complete an application, provide a physician's statement verifying physical health, show proof of current certification (and retain certification through the course of the guide career) in community first aid, CPR, and community water safety through the American Red Cross (or equivalent), among other requirements, and pass a licensing exam. Whitewater rafting/canoeing/kayaking guides need to submit documentation of having completed five trips on each river for which they wish to be licensed. Rock and ice climbing guides must submit a notarized climbing resume.

Other Requirements

Patience, diplomacy, an excellent sense of humor, and the ability to maintain a professional demeanor when faced with stressful situations are keys to success in the job. Occasional encounters with difficult or demanding tour group members is a reality, so patience is more than a virtue for this job, it's a necessity.

Inbound ecotours are usually day or overnight trips, but a certain level of physical fitness, strength, and stamina is still required for certain jobs. Ability to hike, bike, horseback ride, and do other physical activities is usually needed. As a tour guide, you should also be fun loving and able to help group members enjoy themselves. Another important trait is the ability to deal with unforeseen difficulties and situations. Leadership and a take-charge attitude are also necessary in this job, where guides are relied upon to answer

What exactly is an "ecotour"?

The Nature Conservancy and the World Conservation Union define ecotourism as "Environmentally responsible travel to natural areas, in order to enjoy and appreciate nature (and accompanying cultural features, both past and present) that promote conservation, have a low visitor impact, and provide for beneficially active socioeconomic involvement of local peoples."

You know you're on an ecotour if it has the following characteristics:

- Conscientious, low-impact visitor behavior
- Sensitivity toward, and appreciation of, local cultures and biodiversity
- Support for local conservation efforts
- Sustainable benefits to local communities
- Local participation in decision making
- Educational components for both the traveler and local communities

Source: The Nature Conservancy

questions, deal with problems, and generally take care of travelers' needs. Finally, tour guides need to be willing and able to work long hours. During a tour, guides are never really off duty, and this can mean phone calls in the middle of the night to resolve any problem a guest is having. Fluency in a foreign language or two is also extremely beneficial in this type of work. The ability to speak with tourists from other countries improves their tour experience and also helps build relationships that can lead to more business in the future.

EXPLORING

Take a tour yourself to see what tour guides do in their work. Ask them if they have a few minutes to spare after the tour to talk to you about their job and the industry. Bring a list of questions with you so that you'll be sure to have all your questions answered. You can also get firsthand experience by finding a part-time or summer job working as a tour guide. Local museums or historical sites often use part-time workers or volunteers from the community to conduct tours.

EMPLOYERS

Inbound tour guides work for large and small tour companies throughout the country. They may be full-time, salaried staff members, or work part time on a contract basis as need arises. Many own their own companies and create and conduct their own tours. According to the U.S. Department of Labor, in 2006 there were 40,000 tour guides employed in the United States. Some may also work for state departments of conservation and national parks. In addition to leading tours, many guides write and lecture about their experiences to supplement their incomes.

STARTING OUT

Many guides start their careers informally, by choosing day hikes they want to take and leading friends and family on the trips. They may work for outdoor adventure retailers such as Eastern Mountain Sports, which organize their own adventure trips and involve staff members in the excursions. A great way to get started can be through part-time or summer work with these types of stores. You can also search the Internet for opportunities with ecotourism companies. The International Association of Tour Managers—North America also offers a placement service and a job bank that matches tour managers with groups.

ADVANCEMENT

Most guides begin their careers working part time on one-day tours. Until they master the itinerary and information, they often conduct tours with experienced guides. Career advancement can take the form of leading more complicated tours or of specializing in a certain type of tour or destination. Guides who are good at their work often build up a following of repeat customers who sign up for their tours. These popular guides may then be able to move to a higher-paying tour company. Some choose to open agencies of their own.

   Some tour guides become travel writers, reporting on various destinations for the many travel-oriented magazines and newspapers. Others may move into the corporate world, planning travel arrangements for company business travelers.

EARNINGS

Salaries for tour guides vary depending on their level of experience and the regions in which they work. According to the Bureau of Labor Statistics, in 2008 tour guides had median annual earnings of $23,270. The lowest paid 10 percent earned $15,470, annually, and the top paid 10 percent earned $38,280. In 2009 annual salaries for tour guides ranged from $15,000 to $61,000, according to Payscale.com. Guides with one to four years of experience averaged $15,000 to $30,000 annually. Those with five to nine years' work experience earned $23,583 to $42,729 per year. And guides who had been in the business 10 to 19 years had annual salaries ranging from $23,760 to $61,000. In New York, tour guides had median annual salaries of $45,000 in 2009, while Oregon-based tour guides earned lower annual salaries of $32,000, according to Indeed.com statistics.

The work of an inbound tour guide is often seasonal—extremely busy during the peak travel times of May through October, and much slower in the off-season. While traveling, guides receive their meals and accommodations free, as well as a daily stipend to cover additional expenses. They may also receive tips from customers.

Salaried guides may also receive a benefits package that includes sick and vacation time, health insurance, and profit sharing. Additional perks may include discounts from hotels, airlines, and transportation companies.

WORK ENVIRONMENT

Guides have varied work environments, depending on the type of tours they give. Ecotour guides who lead outdoor recreational trips will be in any variety of settings—forests, mountains, parks, lakes, rivers, coastlines, oceans—working in all kinds of weather. Those who lead tours to cities may spend part of their time outdoors walking, as well as indoors in comfortable, clean settings. Those who also give bus and van tours will spend much of their time seated, but will also have to deal with giving running commentary throughout the tour while also paying attention to traffic and road conditions. Work hours will also vary. Some trips will require guides to be accessible 24/7; other trips might take as little as two or three hours of a guide's time. The work hours depend on the nature of the tour.

OUTLOOK

The tour guide industry is directly linked to the economy. In stable times, people have more expendable income and can afford to spend time traveling and exploring. The U.S. Department of Labor forecasts good employment opportunities for tour guides through 2016. Domestic ecotourism is also expanding and may offer more opportunities for guides who have backgrounds in this specialty. Competition for all guide positions will be keen, however, as these jobs are usually extremely popular and highly sought after. Providing the U.S. economy continues along its current recovery and stability tract, the travel and tourism industry should continue to stabilize and grow as well. In addition, the U.S. Department of Commerce predicts an increase in international travel to the United States in the next few years. In 2008, about 58 million international tourists visited the United States. The Department of Commerce predicts this number will increase by 10 percent, to 64 million international visitors, by 2013.

Guides with both cultural and foreign-language skills, especially Russian, German, Spanish, and Japanese, will be in demand. The best opportunities in inbound tourism are in large cities with international airports and in areas with a large amount of tourist traffic. For inbound ecotourism guides, the best opportunities will be in regions near natural areas and environmentally friendly communities and cities.

FOR MORE INFORMATION

Learn more about ecotours by visiting the Web sites of these tour companies.

EcoTours of Oregon
http://www.ecotours-of-oregon.com

Hines Tours Inc.
http://www.hinestours.com

Find job listings and other tour guide information at

International Association of Tour Managers
North American Region
24 Blevins Road, Trails End
Kerhonkson, NY 12446-1302
Tel: 212-208-6800
http://www.tourmanager.org

For background information on the tourism industry and job postings, contact

Travel Industry Association of America
1100 New York Avenue, NW, Suite 450
Washington, DC 20005-3934
Tel: 202-408-8422
http://www.tia.org

For information on the tour industry, contact

United States Tour Operators Association
275 Madison Avenue, Suite 2014
New York, NY 10016-1101
Tel: 212-599-6599
Email: information@ustoa.com
http://www.ustoa.com

Nature Photographers

OVERVIEW

Nature photographers photograph flora and fauna, landscapes, and waterways for art and decorative purposes, commercial use, and for conservation efforts. They work as independent contractors or as salaried employees. Their photographs are used in galleries, museums, and auction houses; various media, including magazines, newspapers, journals, books, and online publications; and in literature and reports published by wildlife and environmental conservation groups.

HISTORY

Nature photography pioneers include Henry Hamilton Bennett, the Kolb brothers, George Shiras III, and Ansel Adams. Henry Hamilton Bennett was an innovator who photographed the Wisconsin Dells area in the second half of the 19th century using cameras he built himself, including stereoscopic cameras. He got into photography after suffering a near-crippling injury to his right hand during the Civil War. In 1902 Emery and Ellsworth Kolb set up their photographic studio at the south rim of the Grand Canyon. They photographed tourists on mules, as they were about to descend the

Bright Angel Trail. The Kolbs would then scramble to develop the film and hike down the mountainside to deliver the photos to visitors as they returned from the river below. (The hike was several miles roundtrip, and they did this numerous times throughout the day!) The Kolb brothers also expanded into nature photography, and became well known for taking great risks to capture images at incredible vantage points.

George Shiras III was the first National Geographic Society wildlife photographer and took the first photographs ever of wildlife at night. As National Geographic explains on its Web site, "Wildlife photography barely existed: Cameras were cumbersome and primitive, wildlife elusive and difficult to film. But Shiras's inventive genius contrived methods and devices that resulted, among other things, in the first flash photographs and the first trip-wire photography of animals at night."

Ansel Adams is famous for his black-and-white photographs of the American West, and Yosemite National Park in particular. He was not only a photographer but also a conservationist who used his work to aid wilderness preservation efforts. For example, his 1938 book *Sierra Nevada: The John Muir Trail*, along with his testimony before Congress, helped the Sierra Club secure the National Park designation to the Sequoia and Kings Canyon area in California in 1940.

THE JOB

Nature photographers take pictures of animals in the wild, flowers and other foliage, butterflies and insects, as well as waterfalls, lakes, ponds, mountains and valleys, and other natural settings. They may specialize in wildlife or in landscape photography, and become known for their work in certain regions or with specific animals. They may photograph nature in their backyard or nearby woods, or travel to remote locations overseas to capture images. Their work may be used for commercial and/or art purposes. Their images appear in print and online, and are used in nature and wildlife magazines, mass-market and trade books, and as promotional and educational literature for conservation groups such as Audubon, Sierra Club, and The Nature Conservancy, among others. They may also exhibit their work in museums, display and sell their work in art galleries and auction houses, and "rent" their images to stock photography agencies.

Wildlife photographers understand how to blend into their surroundings so as not to startle animals in their natural environments.

They are cautious and patient. Some shots may require them to wait a long time for animals to show up at favorite watering holes or lounging spots. And when the animals arrive, photographers are prepared to take pictures immediately because the window of opportunity may not last long. They are also prepared to make hasty retreats, particularly if animals sense intrusion and attack in defense. It's not uncommon for wildlife photo shoots to end with chase scenes through a jungle or savannah, with the tables turned as the photographer and crew become prey. Not all wildlife images require exotic travel, however. Images of animals can also be captured at nature preserves, game farms, or even at zoos.

Nature photographers' pictures may also be used for conservation purposes. Pictures of natural environments such as wetlands and coastlines, and animals such as endangered and threatened species can be used in letter-writing campaigns, call-to-action brochures and e-newsletters, fund-raising calendars, and on conservation organizations' Web sites. Their photographs can also be used by wildlife scientists to study certain animals that are not normally captured and tagged. Nature photographers can capture images of rarely seen animals, particularly those that are most active at night, by setting up "camera traps," which are motion-sensitive cameras hidden in spots animals are known to visit. A camera trap might catch the image of a spotted owl scoring a mouse during an evening hunt, or even a poacher hunting an endangered animal at night.

Nature photographers also photograph seasons in nature, such as trees changing color in autumn, valleys blanketed in winter snow, and frozen ponds thawing in early spring. They may focus their work on a particular region, such as the Adirondacks or Catskills, or on a natural phenomenon such as the Grand Canyon or Niagara Falls. Nature photography is also used for tourism, and is used more increasingly for ecotourism, to promote environments that offer clean air, water, and land, and feature a wide array of interesting wildlife and plant species in healthy surroundings.

Many nature photographers also supplement their incomes through stock photography, which is the licensing of existing stock images. For example, they may go out on assignment for a magazine to shoot elephants in Africa, and take pictures of everything else along the way, which they can sell to stock photo agencies. They deposit images with stock agencies, which search for clients (such as an ad agency that needs a photograph of an elephant herd in Africa) and negotiate image rental agreements. Agencies keep an agreed-upon percentage for arranging the rental of the image, and photographers receive the balance of the money.

A fearless nature photographer gets up close and personal with a 12-foot great white shark. *Barcroft Media via Getty Images*

Photographers work alone or with assistants and photography crews. They use a variety of cameras (from large-format to digital) and equipment (e.g., telephoto lenses, tripods, filters, etc.) in their work. They create packing lists for shoots, to make sure they have everything they need. Another critical aspect of the job is organization. Keeping and recording shot lists and archiving photos systematically are crucial. Photographers need to know photo and archive software. If a client calls asking for a photograph of a tiger in India, as opposed to a tiger in Africa, or even more specifically of an animal yawning or lounging, organized photographers will be able to easily locate these images. They need to be diligent about backing up their material. Self-employed photographers also spend a great deal of time trying to generate business through networking, promotions, advertisements, and marketing.

REQUIREMENTS
High School
Classes that provide a well-rounded foundation for nature photography work include art and photography, art history, general history, computer science (particularly design software programs), math,

Learn More About It

Adams, Ansel. *Ansel Adams: 400 Photographs*. Mill Valley, Calif.: Ansel Adams, 2007.

Bloom, Steve. *Untamed*. New York: Harry N. Abrams, 2004.

Fitzharris, Tim. *National Audubon Society Guide to Landscape Photography*. Tonawanda, N.Y.: Firefly Books, 2007.

Morello, Steven. *The Traveling Nature Photographer: A Guide for Exploring the Natural World Through Photography*. Atglen, Penn.: Schiffer Publishing, 2008.

Shaw, John. *John Shaw's Nature Photography Field Guide*. New York: Amphoto Books, 2001.

Zuckerman, Jim. *Shooting & Selling Your Photographs: The Complete Guide to Making Money with Your Photographs*. Cincinnati, Ohio: Writers Digest Books, 2003.

earth and physical sciences and English. Cultural studies and foreign language classes are also important.

Postsecondary Training

Undergraduate degrees vary for this career. Some photographers have fine arts degrees, others have studied wildlife science, zoology, or even engineering. A science background coupled with arts and photography can be very useful. A college degree is not necessarily required but provides further education on subjects that can benefit photographers in their work. Classes that are helpful include photography, design, wildlife science, ecology, biology, English, communications, business, advertising, marketing, history, cultural studies, and foreign language. Course work in photography design programs, such as Photoshop, is also beneficial.

Other Requirements

A strong visual eye, knowledge of camera equipment and techniques, and attention to detail are required in nature photography. Patience—the ability to quietly wait for the right shots—is important to capture successful photographs in the wild. Survival skills, physical skills, and navigation skills all are critical in this work. Nature photographers need to be self-sufficient and able to solve problems as they arise. Out in the field there may not be a town nearby to replenish supplies or fix broken equipment. Packing for a shoot means considering how much you can carry and what the absolute essentials are, not just for the shoot but also for simple survival. For instance, a shoot in the rainforest means raingear, waders, maps, compasses, medical supplies, on top of cameras and film equipment.

Physical fitness goes with the territory for this kind of work. As one person put it in a photographers' blog, photographers spend "5 percent of their time doing photography, and 95 percent of their time being pack mules." Photographers need to be able to carry camera equipment and gear over rough terrain, sometimes for long periods of time, in any type of weather.

EXPLORING

Read magazines such as *Nature, Audubon, Sierra,* and *National Geographic* to see the subject matter that nature photographers are capturing, and to get a better idea of the images (and regions) that publications' editors are assigning to photographers. Create a list of the photographers' names and google them to find their Web sites. Spend time on their sites, learning more about their professional and educational backgrounds, what inspires them, and how they keep up to date on new technology and techniques. Many nature photographers also enjoy sharing "behind the scenes" commentary on their images—for example, whether it was a carefully planned image or a happy accident, what the weather was like, etc.—which can provide you with further insights into how shots were created.

The Internet also offers blogs and online forums that involve dialogues between professional photographers and photography hobbyists. You can pick up a ton of good advice simply by reading the threads about the pros and cons of nature photography, and all the intricate details involved in starting and running a photography business. Start your search for forums and other networking opportunities through professional associations such as the North American Nature Photography Association and the Nature Photographers Network. (Contact information is located at the end of this article.)

EMPLOYERS

Nature photographers work in full-time positions and as independent contractors for print and online publishing companies, conservation groups, and other organizations that purchase and use nature photography. The Department of Labor reports that in 2006, there were 122,000 photographers employed in the United States, with more than 50 percent working as freelancers. Some freelance photographers have ongoing contracts for photography projects at set fees with magazine publishers or other businesses that use photography. Most salaried photographers work in portrait or commercial photography studios, and for newspapers, magazines, and advertising agencies.

STARTING OUT

Many photographers start out as photographers' assistants. Assisting professional nature photographers who do the type of photography work you want to do is an excellent way to learn the photographic equipment, skills, and techniques needed while you are working on the job. Assisting also provides you with the opportunity to meet other people in the field and make connections for future work referrals. If you can't commit time to an assistant job or an apprenticeship, try to get an internship or part-time job with a nature magazine, nature book publishing company, or a wildlife or habitat conservation center.

You can also learn more about what photography students are doing and talking about, and pick up ideas for new and different shots you can take, by visiting the students section of Nature's Best Photography Web site (http://naturesbeststudents.blogspot.com).

ADVANCEMENT

For many nature photographers, advancement comes from honing photography skills and techniques, and increasing knowledge of specific areas, such as wildlife science, zoology, geology, and cultural studies. Staff photographers may advance to become senior photographers, photography editors, and managing editors of photography departments. They may also advance by branching out into the education field, teaching and lecturing in colleges, universities, and art, photography, and professional schools. They can also advance by moving into other media, such as documentary filmmaking. Many also advance by writing articles, columns, blogs, and books; and by expanding into other markets such as poster and calendar publishing, and stock imagery.

EARNINGS

Salaries for photographers vary widely depending upon type of employment (freelance or staff), and years of experience and reputation in the business. The Bureau of Labor Statistics reports that in 2008 photographers had median annual incomes of $29,440, with salaries ranging from as low as $16,920 to $62,430 or higher. In 2009 nature photographers with one to four years of experience earned $21,498 to $43,650 per year, according to Salary.com.

Freelance nature photographers who have become well known for their work and have multiple income streams (including sales through art galleries, auction houses, and stock imagery agencies) coupled with strong client bases earn higher wages. Many nature photographers are not famous, however, and the ability to earn a respectable, and livable, income in the field is challenging. To stay afloat financially, many hold full-time, salaried jobs in other industries while conducting their freelance nature photography business. They also supplement their incomes through lecturing and teaching, writing articles and books for various media, and submitting their work for stock imagery use.

WORK ENVIRONMENT

There are no set hours for nature photography work. Nature photographers work day or night in all types of weather conditions and climates, and in any number of geographical locations. They may take photographs of glowing jellyfish in oceans at midnight or of desert landscapes at dawn. They may spend long amounts of time in hot, dusty fields, waiting for a herd of animals to show up, or hiking along rushing rivers until they find the spot that "calls" to them. Depending on what they shoot, nature photographers may walk into their backyard, drive to a neighboring town, or fly across the country or around the world to get their shots. They also work in offices, photo labs, and travel to meet with editors and publishers, art gallery owners, museum directors, and stock image managers.

OUTLOOK

Photographers overall can expect employment growth to be as fast as the average through 2016, according to the U.S. Department of Labor (DoL). Photography is an extremely popular career and there are usually far more applicants than available jobs. Salaried positions are especially hard to find because more companies contract freelance photographers for images.

The future of the industry shows a conflicting outlook. On the one hand, the plethora of Internet magazines, journals, and newspapers means increased need for commercial photographers to provide digital images. And better data-management programs make it easier for freelance photographers to market their work directly to customers and rely less on stock photo agencies. On the other hand, because of the development and widespread use of digital photography, more nonprofessionals are promoting themselves as photographers. As the DoL describes it, "Improvements in digital technology reduce barriers of entry into this profession and allow more individual consumers and businesses to produce, store, and access photographic images on their own."

Nature photographers can expect keen competition for salaried work as well as freelance assignments. To improve their marketability, they need to have a strong portfolio, solid knowledge of the subject matter, and excellent communications skills. Those who have special, unique knowledge of their subject matters—such as wildlife science, zoology, or ecology backgrounds, along with a history of field study and research—have better chances of standing out among the job applicant crowd.

FOR MORE INFORMATION

Learn more about the business of being a photographer—including multimedia overviews, pricing and negotiating tips, and legal advice—by visiting

American Society of Media Photographers Inc.
150 North Second Street
Philadelphia, PA 19106-1912
Tel: 215-451-2767
http://asmp.org

Search for nature photographers and find further information about photographers by visiting the "explore art" section of the J. Paul Getty Museum's Web site at

J. Paul Getty Museum
1200 Getty Center Drive
Los Angeles, CA 90049-1679
Tel: 310-440-7330
http://www.getty.edu/art/gettyguide/exploreArt

Find membership information, networking opportunities, workshops, and other resources by visiting the Web sites of the following organizations for nature photographers:

Nature Photographers Network
PO Box 10601
Bedford, NH 03110-0601
Email: editor@naturephotographers.net
http://www.naturephotographers.net

The North American Nature Photography Association
10200 West 44th Avenue, Suite 304
Wheat Ridge, CO 80033-2840
Tel: 303-422-8527
Email: info@nanpa.org
http://www.nanpa.org

Publicists, Green Nonprofit Organizations

QUICK FACTS

School Subjects
Business
English
Marketing

Personal Skills
Communicative/persuasive
Writing

Work Environment
Indoors
One location

Minimum Education Level
Bachelor's degree

Salary Range
$30,140 to $51,280 to
$97,910+

Certification or Licensing
Voluntary

Outlook
Faster than the average

OVERVIEW

Publicists, also known as *public relations specialists, public relations representatives, communications managers* and *communications directors*, help companies build and maintain relationships with the public. Companies hire publicists to help them handle relationships with the press, communities, consumers, industries, and governments. Publicists write company news announcements and press releases, organize speaking engagements and special programs, and prepare publicity and communications materials for different media.

HISTORY

Public relations is a relatively young industry in America, dating to the early 20th century. Rapid consolidation of large, wealthy corporations in the late 1800s gave rise to general mistrust and skepticism of big business by workers and the general public. By the early 1900s, trade unions representing workers emerged, demanding stricter regulations of corporate power. Corporations needed help in improving public opinion and relations with workers. At this time, two men—Ivy Lee and Edward Bernays—innovated what became known as the practice of public relations, or PR.

Ivy Lee had previously been a journalist before handling press relations for railroad companies and the large oil-refining company, Standard Oil. Rather than covering up crises when they occurred—a common response by railroad companies when railway accidents happened—Lee allowed journalists supervised access to accident scenes, an approach that appeased the media and allowed Lee to still have some power over the situation. Lee innovated this "transparent" approach in public relations, but unfortunately, he was not above using lying as a tactic as well. An example is in how he handled the national scandal surrounding the Ludlow Massacre in 1914, in which members of the Colorado National Guard killed striking coal miners and their family members after a long, drawn-out fight. The Guard was working for John D. Rockefeller, owner of the Ludlow mine in Colorado. Lee spun the story on Rockefeller's behalf, claiming the miners had set fire to their tents (when it had been the National Guard) and that it was the miners who had provoked the attack (when they had not).

Edward Bernays, a nephew of Sigmund Freud, honed his public relations skills in his work for Woodrow Wilson's pro-war propaganda outfit, the Committee for Public Information (or the Creel Commission), which aimed to bolster American public support for U.S. involvement in World War I. Bernays opened his own public relations business in New York after the war, and worked for various companies, including CBS, General Electric, and Proctor & Gamble. Bernays applied social psychology theories to his mass communication work. He is well remembered for his success in boosting tobacco sales in the 1930s for his client Chesterfield cigarettes, by positioning smoking as a symbol of emancipation for feminists at that time.

Public relations expanded in the 1940s and 1950s, with larger companies emerging in the United States, such as Burson-Marsteller and Hill & Knowlton. These organizations established offices across the country as well as overseas, making it easier to organize and run international public relations campaigns. In the 1960s lobbying became another PR service, introduced by Hill & Knowlton. Today, public affairs and government relations are standard services offered by many PR agencies. Since the 1960s most of the major public relations companies have merged with other companies or been bought out by larger organizations. While the business structure, tools, and technologies have changed over time, public relations continues to be used for multiple reasons, including to influence legislation, improve companies' reputations, attract investments, clear up disasters, encourage support for political campaigns, and educate the public about issues that affect their lives and environment.

THE JOB

A publicist's job is to help companies appear in the best light possible, to get word out about its good deeds, and to clarify and explain things if public information is misconstrued or negative events have occurred. An organization's reputation can make or break its business—it's up to publicists to help companies manage their communications, ensuring that details of their mission, programs and products, finances, board members and staff, and policies are conveyed accurately and honestly. When an organization is under the spotlight for a particular issue or activity, a publicist helps the organization strategize the best ways to manage the communications—internally, to staff and to the organization's members; and externally, to the industry at large, the media, and the general public.

Publicists who work for green nonprofit organizations have the same core tasks as publicists at for-profit organizations—to make sure their clients receive optimum press coverage, and ensure that the coverage is positive. Developing and maintaining relationships with the media is a key element to a publicist's success. Publicists invest a great deal of time in establishing working relationships with reporters, editors, and TV news producers. A portion of their days is allocated to networking with members of the press—through telephone calls, email exchanges, and in-person meetings. They put in long hours, and their workdays don't end at 5:00 P.M. If there is a media gathering on a Tuesday night or a conference that runs through the weekend, and it offers the opportunity to interact with influential journalists, publicists will be there.

While it is no longer the sole tool in a publicist's repertoire, the press release still carries weight. In earlier days of the public relations industry, press releases were either faxed or mailed; today, news announcements are made by email, as well as through social media networks such as Twitter and Facebook. Press releases are written in a style similar to news articles, with attention-grabbing headlines and the most important information at the top of the piece (as in the "pyramid" approach). For Twitter and similar networks, space is limited, so the ability to write concise, engaging copy is essential.

Publicists help companies decide what is and is not newsworthy and on which issues and areas of the company to focus their communication messages. Green publicists write press releases and news announcements ("tweets" on Twitter) to inform the public about the nonprofit organization's progress in addressing certain issues, or when the organization succeeds in certain areas. For example, a publicist will write and send an announcement about the organization's success in securing funding to create an educational program for kids, or if the company is succeeding in helping to clean up and restore a wetland area. Announcements and press releases can also tell the general public about action the organization is taking on certain issues, such as lobbying in Washington, D.C., for specific environmental policy changes or new laws. Publicists send press releases to their contacts at newspapers, magazines, TV news networks, government agencies, other nonprofit organizations, as well as to staff and organization members and donors.

Publicists also handle organizations' Web site content and print and online publications, and depending on the organization, they may also help in other program areas. For example, Tom Andersen, director of communications at Westchester Land Trust, coordinates the organization's communications and grants program, and oversees the land acquisition and easement program. Westchester Land Trust, headquartered in Bedford Hills, N.Y., works with private land owners to protect Westchester County's lands and communities through conservation easements—legal agreements that restrict future development on lands that have conservation value, such as wildlife habitats or scenic open spaces. Tom's job entails managing the Web site, writing and editing the newsletter and publications, as well as writing grant proposals and helping to outline the programs for which they seek funding. To date he has succeeded in securing more than two dozen grants for vital land preservation programs. He also writes and sends out one to two emails per month to supporters of the organization; handles relations with the press, including writing press releases, handling press calls, and initiating press coverage; and oversees the social media strategy, using Twitter and Facebook.

Other aspects of publicists' jobs include setting up speaking engagements and preparing speeches for company officials; helping to create films, videos, slides, or other video presentations for the Internet and Web, and for meetings and presentations; and planning and coordinating conferences and conventions. Publicists also research, write, and prepare materials regarding company policies and programs, and respond to email and telephone inquiries. They may also be responsible for creating annual reports and writing proposals for projects.

REQUIREMENTS
High School
Publicists have a variety of backgrounds, but the one skill they all share is strong writing ability. Take English and writing classes to hone these skills. And round out your education with course work in math, science (biology, ecology, geology), environmental studies (if your school offers this), history, computer software programs, and foreign language.

Postsecondary Training
An undergraduate degree in a communications-related field is usually required to work as a publicist. Many organizations may require advanced degrees coupled with related work experience. Publicists have degrees in public relations, journalism, advertising, or communication. Green nonprofit publicists may have combined degrees in journalism and environmental science, or a specialty that relates to the nonprofit organization's mission. Courses in advertising, marketing, political science, sociology, psychology, business administration, and finance provide a solid basis for future public relations work. Course work in environmental policy and legislation is also particularly useful in the green nonprofit sector.

Certification or Licensing
Certification in the public relations field is voluntary. Many colleges and universities that offer public relations degree programs also offer certification programs through continuing education departments. New York University, for example, offers public relations certification through its School of Continuing and Professional Studies. Publicists who meet specific requirements and pass an examination can also receive the Accredited Business Communicator designation from the International Association of Business Communicators.

Other Requirements
Strong verbal and written communication skills are required to do publicity work. Successful publicists are detail oriented, organized, decisive, and energetic. A positive attitude helps in handling the many stresses that come with the territory. Work hours can

sometimes be long, and things don't always go as planned. Publicists are available at all hours to address last-minute changes to schedules, or help resolve emergencies or crises. Many public relations positions require knowledge of software programs such as Microsoft Word and Excel, as well as design programs such as Adobe InDesign and Illustrator.

EXPLORING

You can hone your writing and speaking skills by volunteering to write for your school's newspaper and participating in the debate team or other speaking clubs at your school. Also take advantage of resources available through professional associations. For example, visit the career center of the Council of Public Relations Firms' Web site (http://www.prfirms.org) to read articles about careers in public relations, and peruse the job listings section to learn more job descriptions and the types of companies that are hiring public relations specialists. Tom Andersen also recommends staying up to speed on current communications methods. He says, "My best advice is to use all the new ways we have of communicating and networking, move on to new methods as they appear, and be prepared to use them or whatever else has evolved in five or 10 years when you're ready to get a job."

EMPLOYERS

In 2006 approximately 243,000 public relations specialists were employed in the United States. Numerous and various green nonprofit organizations employ publicists to help them manage their public relations. Conservation groups, advocacy organizations, sustainability consultants, and environmental education groups employ public relations specialists. Publicists may also work for public relations and communications firms that specialize in handling public relations for green nonprofit organizations. According to the U.S. Department of Labor, many public relations firms are concentrated in New York, Los Angeles, San Francisco, Chicago, and Washington, D.C.

STARTING OUT

Publicists start their careers in a variety of ways. Many have prior writing and editing experience. Before joining the staff of Westchester Land Trust, Tom Andersen had worked as a reporter for 17 years for the *Journal News* in Westchester, where he covered the environment and politics. His previous communications experience also includes positions with Purchase College, the New York State Assembly, and the Lake Placid Winter Olympics. Interning with a publicist or in the public relations department of a green nonprofit organization is an excellent way to get started in the field and learn more about public relations. There are plenty of organizations that work with public relations specialists—even green markets and farmers' markets need publicity help. Contact green nonprofit organizations in your area to see if they need extra part-time or summer publicity help. You may also be able to find opportunities through the Public Relations Society of America.

ADVANCEMENT

Publicists may start their careers as research assistants or account coordinators and advance to the next level of account executive. With experience, they can move up to become senior account executives, account managers, and eventually vice presidents. Titles will vary depending on the organization's structure. Salaried publicists may leave full-time positions to start their own consulting firms.

Many publicists maintain freelance writing careers while working and consulting full time. They write books and articles on subjects they are most passionate and concerned about. For instance, Tom Andersen authored the book *This Fine Piece of Water: An Environmental History of Long Island Sound*, and he continues to write and lecture about Long Island Sound issues while working for the Westchester Land Trust.

EARNINGS

Annual salaries for public relations specialists ranged from $30,140 to $97,910 in 2008, with average median incomes of about $51,280, as reported in the *Occupational Outlook Handbook*. Salaries vary depending on the industry and employer; in general, salaries are lower in the nonprofit sector than in the for-profit industry. Public relations specialists who worked for advertising, public relations, and related services had annual salaries of $67,960, while those who worked for business, professional, labor, political, and similar organizations earned $64,310. Public relations specialists who worked for local governments or for colleges, universities, and professional schools had salaries that were on the low end of the scale in 2008: $53,070 (government), and $50,690 (schools). The top five states where the most jobs for public relations specialists can be found are the District of Columbia, Colorado, New York, Massachusetts, and Vermont.

WORK ENVIRONMENT

Publicists usually work more than 40 hours per week. They need to be accessible at all times to handle situations as soon as they arise. They may need to work late one night to write a speech for a press conference that was scheduled at the last minute. Or, they may have to attend a weekend event that their organization or client is hosting. Hours will be long, and publicists must have flexibility to adjust their schedules to meet demands and deadlines. They generally work in offices, and travel for client meetings, conferences, and events.

OUTLOOK

Employment growth in the public relations industry is expected to be faster than the average through 2016. More companies are contracting external public relations help rather than hiring staff. As a result, independent consultants who own their own businesses are expected to have better employment opportunities than those seeking full-time, salaried positions. Publicity jobs are extremely popular—if this field interests you, prepare for keen competition in the job market. Publicists with excellent communication skills, many (and solid) press contacts, and a proven track record with reputable organizations are highly desired by employers.

FOR MORE INFORMATION

Find career information and other resources for public relations professionals at
Council of Public Relations Firms
317 Madison Avenue, Suite 2320
New York, NY 10017-5205
Tel: 877-773-4767
http://www.prfirms.org

Learn more about accreditation in communications by visiting
International Association of Business Communicators
601 Montgomery Street, Suite 1900
San Francisco, CA 94111-2623

Tel: 800-776-4222
http://www.iabc.com

Find information about networking opportunities, workshops, job listings, and publications by visiting
Public Relations Society of America
33 Maiden Lane, 11th Floor
New York, NY 10038-5150
http://www.prsa.org

Science Writers

QUICK FACTS

School Subjects
English
Math
Science

Personal Skills
Communication/writing
Helping/teaching

Work Environment
Indoors and outdoors
One or more locations

Minimum Education Level
Bachelor's degree

Salary Range
$28,020 to $53,070 to
$106,030+

Certification or Licensing
Not required

Outlook
About as fast as the average

OVERVIEW

Science writers write about a wide range of science topics for magazines, newspapers, journals, and mass-market and trade publishers. They also write scripts for films, documentaries, videos, and other media. They may write about general science topics, or specialize in any number of scientific areas, such as ecology, biochemistry, or environmental science. Their work involves conducting research, identifying and interviewing sources, writing and editing copy, and working closely with editors.

HISTORY

The first two scientific journals were published in 1665—*Journal des Scavans*, a French journal covering a wide range of knowledge; and the Royal Society of London's *Philosophical Transactions*, a more specifically scientific publication, although "science" in those days was better known as "natural philosophy." *Transactions* was published monthly and featured works by such great minds as Isaac Newton, famous for coming up with the three laws of motion, among countless other contributions to science; Anton van Leeuwenhoek, considered to be the "father of microscopy" for advances he made in microscope design and use; and Robert Boyle, regarded as the founder of modern chemistry, noted particularly for his study of the mechanics of air. Other early scientists featured in *Transactions* were Robert Hooke, who was the first to record and study cells under a microscope, and Edmund Halley, famous for analyzing the orbits of comets.

The scientific journal publishing field grew in the 17th and 18th centuries. In the early days, journals generally included compilations of papers and writings lifted from other journals, as well as summaries of newly published scientific books. By the start of the 20th century, thousands of scientific journals were being published, and the general population was taking a greater interest in science. As the science field became more professionalized, more periodicals were established that focused on explaining science to readers who did not have scientific backgrounds. The publication *Nature* was established in 1869, with a mission "to ensure that the results of science are rapidly disseminated to the public throughout the world, in a fashion that conveys their significance for knowledge, culture and daily life." *Science*, a weekly academic journal of the American Association for the Advancement of Science, was also introduced in the late 1800s. Like *Nature*, it is a peer-reviewed journal that publishes original scientific research, reviews, and analyses.

Today, readers of different age groups, educational levels, and professional and cultural backgrounds can access science news and information through a wide range of media—from print publications to blogs and podcasts. Scientific journals continue to proliferate, as do mainstream publications that cover broad areas of science for the nonscientific reader.

THE JOB

Science writers write articles and content for scientific journals, mass-market and specialized magazines, consumer and trade book publishers, as well as for nonprofit organizations and government agencies for use in newsletters, brochures, reports, and films, videos, and Web sites. Science writers may cover topics for audiences of scientists, a job that usually requires professional scientific background and training in order to convey complex material. They may also gear their work to readers with nonscientific backgrounds, which requires translating complex material into language readers can grasp.

Science writers are either assigned topics to cover by editors or they choose subject matter that interests them and is timely, such as

Science writers must sometimes spend time in the field conducting research and studying topics relevant to their current project. *AP Photo/Richmond Times-Dispatch, Rex Springston*

the discovery of a new species or a breakthrough in genetic research. It should also be noted that science writing is distinctly different from environmental journalism. Science writers write about science research and analyses; they will also write about environmental research, but it is the environmental journalist's job to cover environmental regulations and policies.

As the Council for the Advancement of Science Writing explains it, "Science writers' work is important because they remain the chief conduit between scientists and the public. Their reporting not only can bring exciting news of remarkable scientific achievements, but also inform the public about critical issues to aid public debate on areas of science involving ethics and policy questions, for example. Science writers also provide the scientific background on breaking news from earthquakes to oil spills and alert the public to medical and environmental dangers."

Science writers collect data for their articles from a wide range of sources, including journal articles, specialized books, and research reports, to write pieces for journals geared to scientists, physicians, and engineers. Many travel to participate in research projects and expeditions, and write about what they learn. They may translate scientific information for mass-market magazines, television, and news Web sites—a sector of the science writing industry known as "popular science," which literally means "popularizing science," making it more accessible to the general population. On the other side of the spectrum, science writers may also be professional scientists working in the field and writing about subjects they are studying and projects on which they are working. Science writers work in full-time, salaried positions for publications and scientific services organizations and associations. They also work as freelancers, conceiving story ideas, pitching articles to and receiving assignments from newspapers, magazines, and other media.

REQUIREMENTS
High School
Science and writing classes provide a solid foundation for future science writing work. Take classes in biology, ecology, geology, chemistry, environmental science, English, writing, math, history, social science, and computers. If your school offers any classes related to animals, take these as well. Art and photography classes are also extremely useful, particularly since many science writers need knowledge of multimedia for their work.

Postsecondary Training
Science writers may have science and/or journalism degrees. Those who major in science must still hone interviewing and writing skills, and journalism majors need to take science classes to understand the scientific approach, concepts, and terms. Other useful classes while in school include environmental science and studies, communications and mass media, writing and English, computer software programs, and environmental policy and regulations.

Other Requirements
At heart, all science writers share the same trait: curiosity. They got into the field to begin with because they enjoy digging deeper into scientific topics and learning more, and they eagerly share this knowledge with readers. Science writers not only *write* a great deal, but they also *read* tons of information. Research is the foundation for the work. They need to have excellent communication skills to interview various scientists and translate material into language that readers can understand. Writers are also not afraid to ask questions. Scientific topics can be complex, and if writers don't understand something, they keep asking questions to ensure they get things

Science Writing:
It's Writing, and Then Some...

A large aspect of science writing is sitting down at the computer and stringing sentences together—the goal being to create content that engages and educates readers. But before the sitting and stringing together begins, research is needed. And it can be done in many ways, and in many combinations of ways, including by interviewing scientists, reading books and journals, watching films and attending lectures, and also literally getting out into field. For Wendee Holtcamp, a Houston-based freelance science writer, exploring nature is intrinsic to her job, and it runs deep in her DNA.

Wendee got her love for wildlife, nature, and the great outdoors from growing up in a rustic log cabin in the Oregon woods with a "hippie dad, no running water, an outhouse, and wood stoves for cooking." Wendee covers conservation, wildlife, and adventure travel, and she writes for a myriad of media, including Animal Planet and Discovery Channel Online (http://blogs.discovery.com/animal_news). She loves "tromping around swamps in rubber waders, catching frogs snakes, or gators, but is equally comfortable giving professional seminars or teaching biology or her online writing classes." And adventures? She has had plenty. She dove with sharks in Australia's Coral Sea in 2008 during the filming of "Mysteries of the Shark Coast" for Discovery Channel's Shark Week blog (http://blogs.discovery.com/expedition_shark). For *National Wildlife Magazine*, she trekked through the Himalayan foothills of Nepal in search of endangered red pandas. Other expeditions include an assignment for *Global Traveler Magazine* in which she traveled to the Peruvian Amazon, and for *E/The Environmental Magazine*, she wrote about carbon-neutral cruises that people may take to view wildlife of the Galapagos Islands. She has also written for *Scientific American*, *Smithsonian*, *OnEarth*, *Audubon*, *Sierra*, and other magazines.

Wendee earned an MS in wildlife ecology from Texas A&M University and was a National Science Foundation Graduate Research Fellow. In addition to blogging, writing articles, and teaching, she is also currently writing her first book, which is about making peace between evolution and Christianity. You can follow Wendee's travels and learn more about the science topics she covers by visiting http://www.wendeeholtcamp.com.

right. The ability to listen closely and carefully is important, and attention to detail is essential. Skill in working with multimedia has also become essential in the field—such as using text, graphics, video, and audio to share articles.

EXPLORING

Science writers read everything they can get their hands on—journals, magazines, books, newspapers. Follow their lead and read science magazines such as *Scientific American* and *Popular Science*. Keep up with science trends and news by regularly visiting Web sites such as Science News (http://www.sciencenews.org) and Science Daily (http://www.sciencedaily.com). Professional associations also offer plenty of useful resources for beginning writers. Explore the Web sites of such organizations as the National Association of Science Writers, the World Federation of Science Journalists, and the American Society of Journalists and Authors. (Contact information is located at the end of this article.)

EMPLOYERS

Science writers work full time or on a contract basis for magazines, newspapers, consumer and academic book publishers, professional associations, conservation groups, and public information offices of companies, universities, and hospitals. They also work for Internet news service companies, television networks and film and documentary production companies, and scientific organizations that publish newsletters, magazines, brochures, and Internet content.

The Bureau of Labor Statistics reports that there were 306,000 writers and editors employed in the United States in 2006. About 33 percent of all writers worked in the information sector, which included newspaper and book publishers, Internet publishing and broadcasting, and radio and television broadcasting, among others. Many also worked in professional, scientific, and technical services, and public and private educational services.

STARTING OUT

Science writers may have backgrounds as professional scientists. Many also have prior work experience as reporters or educators, covering other subject areas before becoming interested in focusing on science topics. You can get your start in this career by honing your writing skills now. Assign yourself an article on a subject that interests you, research and interview sources, and write the piece. If you have your own Web site, you can post your writing there or even start a blog. You can also submit your articles to your school newspaper, local newspapers, or other media that publish science-related writing. Be sure to also read the article "Starting a Career in Science Writing," by Andrew Fazekas and Jim Austin, for insights into the field. You can locate it in the careers section of *Science* magazine's Web site (http://sciencecareers. sciencemag.org/career_development/previous_issues/articles/ 3570/starting_a_career_in_science_writing).

ADVANCEMENT

Science writers advance in any number of ways, depending upon their interests. If they typically write articles and shorter pieces for newspapers and magazines, they may explore writing books. They may also branch out into films and documentaries, writing and editing scripts and participating in film shoots. They may teach and lecture about the science specialization they cover, or they may help others learn how to write about science; for example, in addition to providing writing services for clients, Wendee Holtcamp also offers online writing workshops to beginning science writers.

Science writers who work on staff in editorial departments at magazines may move up to become senior writers, senior editors, or managing editors. Staff writers may also advance by starting their own writing and consulting businesses, and teaching at colleges, universities, and professional associations.

EARNINGS

In 2008 writers and authors averaged $53,070 per year, with the lowest paid 10 percent earning $28,020 and the top paid 10 percent averaging $106,030 or more annually, according to the Bureau of Labor Statistics. Newspaper, periodical, book, and directory publishers paid lower salaries ($51,980) to writers and authors. Those who worked for radio and television broadcasting in 2008 had slightly higher salaries ($63,330), and writers who worked for management, scientific, and technical consulting services fared even better ($84,520 annually). SimplyHired.com reports the average annual income for science writers was $56,000 in 2009. Salaries usually vary by level of experience and region. For instance, science writers in Washington, D.C., had median annual incomes of $75,000 in 2009, according to SimplyHired.com. New York-based science writers earned about $66,000 per year, while science writers in Kansas averaged $50,000 annually and North Dakota writers grossed about $47,000 per year.

WORK ENVIRONMENT

Science writers work in offices, classrooms, and out in the field researching and studying the topics they're covering. Their work may take them to labs to interview scientists, or to oceans across the world to study and write about coral reefs. The job can be hectic, involving travel, deadline pressure, and sometimes overwhelming amounts of work, but it can also be stimulating and exciting. The work offers opportunities to explore the world, meet new people from different cultures and backgrounds, and learn about scientific developments and breakthroughs.

OUTLOOK

The future looks bright for science writers, but competition will be keen because this is a popular career. Writers with master's or doctoral degrees coupled with excellent writing skills and solid knowledge of scientific topics will have better chances of securing work. The U.S. Department of Labor (DoL) predicts employment growth for writers and editors in general will grow about as fast as the average for all occupations through 2016. Professional, scientific, and technical service firms are growing, which will offer science writers more employment opportunities in the coming years. Writers will also be needed for Web-based publications, and for blogging and other interactive media. Print magazines are also continuing to develop online content and will need writers to provide articles. The DoL expects writers with training in a specialized field to fare best in the job market. More people are interested in understanding scientific developments and technologies, and in learning more about environmental science topics. Writers who are skilled at translating scientific, technological, and legal material for a more general audience will be in demand.

FOR MORE INFORMATION

Learn more about membership and find useful writing resources at the following organizations' Web sites:

American Society of Journalists and Authors
1501 Broadway, Suite 302
New York, NY 10036-5505

Tel: 212-997-0947
http://www.asja.org

Council for the Advancement of Science Writing
PO Box 910
Hedgesville, WV 25427-0910
Tel: 304-754-6786
http://casw.org

National Association of Science Writers Inc.
PO Box 7905
Berkeley, CA 94707-0905
Tel: 510-647-9500
http://www.nasw.org

Find information about courses, conferences, and internships and job postings by visiting
World Federation of Science Journalists
28 Caron Street
Gatineau (QC), Canada J8Y 1Y7
Tel: 819-770-0776
Email: info@wfsj.org
http://www.wfsj.org

Transportation Planners

QUICK FACTS

School Subjects
Environmental studies
Math

Personal Skills
Analytical/technical
Communication/ideas

Work Environment
Primarily indoors
One location

Minimum Education Level
Bachelor's degree

Salary Range
$37,960 to $59,810 to
$91,520+

Certification or Licensing
None required

Outlook
Faster than the average

OVERVIEW

Transportation planners work for transportation departments of government agencies and engineering companies to strategize transportation plans that reduce the impact on the environment. Their work involves researching and analyzing streets, roads, highways, traffic flow, public transportation, air transportation, rail, and freight. They may also participate in and lead public forums and workshops to educate government employees, policymakers, and the general public about transportation issues and projects.

HISTORY

Global concerns about climate change and the need to reduce carbon emissions have caused many communities and cities to create and promote more sustainable transportation systems. Sustainable transportation usually includes human-powered transport, such as walking, biking, skateboarding, roller skating, etc.; hybrid and electric buses, cars, scooters, and motorcycles; and vehicles powered by renewable energy, such as solar, wind, and water. Public transportation has historically been positioned as a way for people to save money and hassle by leaving their cars at home. Recently, mass transit systems have been promoted as green transportation. Yet what falls under the umbrella of green transportation is often debatable, with some modes of travel being "greener" than others. For example, if everyone takes the traditional diesel bus to work every day, it will harm the environment less than if each person commutes alone in his or her individual car. Still, the hybrid electric-powered bus is the greener public transit option. More cities are incorporating these cleaner running buses into their systems.

Other actions that have been taken to help reduce air and land pollution include the creation and improvement of bicycle paths and walkways, along with development and expansion of parks and open space areas. According to SustainLane.com, a Web site that provides surveys that rank cities on their sustainability practices (including their offerings and quality of green transportation), the top five green cities in the United States in 2008 were Portland, Oregon; San Francisco, California; Seattle, Washington; Chicago, Illinois; and, believe it or not, New York, New York, which, due to public transit use, smaller homes, and densely packed buildings, has one-third fewer per capita emissions than the rest of the country. Other ways to rank cities as green include a city's walkability and bike-ablilty, and overall usage of public transportation and carpooling. Many cities are featuring information on their Web sites about their green transportation systems and plans, as well as special events to promote cleaner modes of travel.

THE JOB

Transportation planners help governments create and implement environmentally friendly transportation plans. They research and assess the effects of transportation on local environments and brainstorm ways to reduce air, land, water, and/or noise pollution and other damage. Their work may involve designing new infrastructures or improving upon existing structures and facilities. Transportation factors they take into account can include traffic junctures, pedestrian walkways, bicycle paths, bus stops, train stations, parking areas, and car-free zones.

Transportation planners work closely with government officials at the local, state, and federal levels, as well as with consultants, on transportation projects. They may conduct surveys as well as research and analyze existing data related to roadways, traffic flow, public transportation options, air transportation, trains, freight, and non-motorized transportation. They study the effects of various transportation methods on the environment and write reports and make presentations regarding their findings and recommendations to government officials and the general public. They are skilled in interpreting and analyzing complex data, understanding and applying transportation planning guidelines, and using spreadsheet and database software and computer-aided design software in their work.

A 2009 job posting for a transportation director with a U.S. city council called for an experienced planner to work on long-range transportation issues. Responsibilities included developing population projections, maps, and financial forecasts for the long-range transportation plan, and analyzing the effects of the plan on the environment and society. On a daily basis, the transportation director would handle non-motorized transportation issues, which could include meeting with local governments regarding bicycle and pedestrian facilities; reviewing grant requests in relation to green transportation plans and projects; and assisting local organizations in securing more grant funding for projects. Other responsibilities included organizing workshops to inform local organizations about non-motorized transportation issues affecting the region, overseeing and managing consultants assigned to work on grant projects for non-motorized transportation, and working with federal and state officials to "advocate for user-friendly policies for non-motorized users on state facilities in the area." The transportation director was expected to liaise with the regional transit agency, and coordinate public involvement in the transportation planning process, which included staging public announcements and appearances, organizing public meetings, giving presentations, and educating the general public about transportation issues.

Transportation planners also deal with environmental documentation relating to the National Environmental Policy Act (NEPA) and the state's Environmental Quality Act; for instance, in California, planners handle documentation that relates to CEQA (California Environmental Quality Act). They make sure transportation plans are in compliance with these acts, and may also conduct environmental assessments and field studies for large transportation projects. They analyze travel data and accident records, and use computer simulation models to examine and compare the effects of different road improvements over the long term. They may act as expert witnesses at public inquiries and transportation planning appeals, and write bids for funding of certain transportation plans.

Two transportation planners from Alaska testify before a Disaster Recovery Subcommittee field hearing regarding coastal erosion. *AP Photo/Al Grillo*

REQUIREMENTS
High School
Transportation planners rely on strong math skills in their work. Be sure to take classes in algebra, geometry and trigonometry. Environmental studies classes are also useful, as is course work in social studies, history, English, computer science, and a foreign language.

Postsecondary Training
Many travel planners have undergraduate degrees in urban planning, transportation engineering, or environmental engineering. They may also have backgrounds in civil and industrial engineering. Classes that are particularly useful are statistics, calculus, and physics. Some employers may require planners to have a masters or doctoral degree in transportation planning. Specialties may include transportation systems engineering, transportation planning, transportation economics, and transportation science.

Other Requirements

Transportation planners are keenly interested in finding transportation solutions that work more harmoniously with the environment. Successful planners are problem solvers who have thorough knowledge of transportation and travel issues within the city in which they work. They also have an awareness of the transportation issues that other cities and countries face and the solutions they have come up with. Strong knowledge of environmental issues and federal, state, and local environmental rules and regulations is also required to succeed in the job. Transportation planners must be detail oriented, able to juggle projects and meet deadlines, work well independently and on teams, and be well versed in a variety of spreadsheet, database, and computer-aided design software programs. The ability to work with a variety of people—staff members, government officials, the media, and the general public—is also crucial.

EXPLORING

The easiest way to learn more about a city's efforts toward providing greener transportation is to visit its Web site and look for the transportation and visitors sections. The green transportation planner field is relatively new and still evolving. Exploring the field at this early stage involves gathering knowledge about green transportation options and developments, attending conferences and lectures about green transportation, and learning more about the cities and communities that are offering innovative travel options to accommodate environmentally concerned travelers. Books about transportation planning also offer deeper insights into issues and solutions. Two useful ones to start with include *An Introduction to Sustainable Transportation: Policy, Planning, and Implementation*, by Preston L. Schiller, Eric Braun, and Jeffrey R. Kenworthy; and *Sustainable Transportation: Problems and Solutions*, by William R. Black.

EMPLOYERS

According to the Bureau of Labor Statistics, there were about 34,000 urban and regional planners (including transportation planners) employed in the United States in 2006. The majority work for local governments. Many planners also work in the private sector for companies that provide management, scientific, and technical consulting services. Others work for state and regional transportation companies, and some work for the federal government.

STARTING OUT
A part-time or summer job with your city's transportation department or with an organization that provides environmental transportation services is the best way to gain exposure to this type of work. Visit your city's department of transportation Web site to search for job openings and internships. You may also find job listings by visiting the Web sites of professional associations such as the Institute of Transportation Engineers (http://www.ite.org) and the American Planning Association, Transportation Planning Division (http://www.apa-tpd.org).

ADVANCEMENT
Transportation planners within government agencies may advance by taking on more responsibilities and handling larger, more complex transportation planning projects. With years of experience, they may move up to management positions such as senior transportation planner or department head. They may expand their knowledge by securing advanced degrees. They may also advance by lecturing and teaching in colleges and universities, and by writing books and articles about green transportation planning.

EARNINGS
Transportation planners' salaries vary according to level of experience and geographic location. The annual salary for an open environmental transportation planner position in Irvine, California, was $70,000, according to a 2009 posting on the employment site Get Civil Engineering Jobs (http://www.getcivilengineeringjobs.com). A posting on the site KansasCityHelpWanted.com showed that the salary being offered in 2009 for a transportation planner with the City of Ames, in Kansas City, Missouri, ranged from $48,518 to $70,932, depending upon work experience and qualifications. According to the Department of Labor, urban and regional planners had median annual incomes of $59,810 in 2008; salaries ranged from $37,960 to $91,520 or higher. The top paying states for this industry were the District of Columbia, Nevada, California, Illinois, and New Jersey.

WORK ENVIRONMENT

Transportation planners work 40 or more hours per week. They sometimes work in the evenings and weekends when projects are nearing deadlines. They also attend public hearings with citizens' groups, which are often scheduled after business hours. Transportation planners generally work in offices, but will spend some time out of the office to research and inspect sites that transportation plans and studies are focused on. They juggle multiple projects and deal with a wide variety of people. Occasionally, transportation projects can incite heated debate among public interest groups and government agencies. Transportation planners need to stay focused on the details while handling the stress professionally and diplomatically in order to succeed in the job.

OUTLOOK

The career outlook for transportation planners is bright. Those with advanced degrees and strong computer skills will have improved odds of securing work. The Department of Labor (DoL) forecasts faster than average employment growth for urban and regional planners through 2016. The growing population will place greater demand on transportation needs. This, coupled with requirements to create transportation methods that meet stricter environmental laws and regulations, will contribute to the growth of employment opportunities for transportation planners. The DoL also predicts that nongovernmental initiatives regarding historic preservation and redevelopment will also create employment growth. Job opportunities will also arise from the need to replace planners who leave for other positions or retire from the field.

FOR MORE INFORMATION

Find job listings and other resources by visiting the following organizations' Web sites:

American Planning Association
Transportation Planning Division
http://www.apa-tpd.org

Institute of Transportation Engineers
1099 14th Street, NW, Suite 300
Washington, DC 20005-3438

Tel: 202-289-0222
http://www.ite.org

Learn more about public transportation issues by visiting
American Public Transportation Association
1666 K Street, NW, Suite 1100
Washington, DC 20006-2803
Tel: 202-496-4800
http://www.apta.com

Find rankings for and descriptions of green U.S. cities by visiting
Sustain Lane
http://www.sustainlane.com

Further Reading

Adams, Ansel. *Ansel Adams: 400 Photographs*. Mill Valley, Calif.: Ansel Adams, 2007.

Adams, Sally. *Interviewing for Journalists (Media Skills)*. New York: Routledge, 2009.

Andersen, Tom. *This Fine Piece of Water: An Environmental History of Long Island Sound*. New Haven, Conn.: Yale University Press, 2002.

Aronson, Merry, et al. *The Public Relations Writer's Handbook: The Digital Age*. Hoboken, N.J.: Jossey-Bass, 2007.

Barbato, Joseph, and Danielle Furlitch. *Writing for a Good Cause*. New York: Fireside, 2000.

Bloom, Steve. *Untamed*. New York: Harry N. Abrams, 2004.

Blum, Deborah, et al, eds. *A Field Guide for Science Writers: The Official Guide of the National Association of Science Writers*. New York: Oxford University Press, 2005.

Bray, Ilona. *Effective Fundraising for Nonprofits: Real-World Strategies that Work*. Berkeley, Calif.: NOLO, 2008.

Brown, Larissa Golden, and Martin John Brown. *Demystifying Grant Seeking: What You Really Need to Do to Get Grants*. Hoboken, N.J.: Jossey-Bass, 2001.

Buckingham, Susan. *Understanding Environmental Issues*. Thousand Oaks, Calif.: Sage Publications Ltd, 2008.

Buckley, Ralf. *Ecotourism: Principles and Practices*. Oxford, England: CABI, 2009.

Buell, Lawrence. *The Future of Environmental Criticism: Environmental Crisis and Literary Imagination*. Hoboken, N.J.: Wiley-Blackwell, 2005.

Burroughs, John. *Signs and Seasons*. Syracuse, N.Y.: Syracuse University Press, 2006.

Carson, Rachel. *Silent Spring*. New York: Mariner Books, 2002.

Corbett, Julia B. *Communicating Nature: How We Create and Understand Environmental Messages*. Washington, D.C.: Island Press, 2006.

Cronin, John, and Robert Kennedy. *The Riverkeepers: Two Activists Fight to Reclaim Our Environment as a Basic Human Right*. New York: Scribner, 1999.

Crutchfield, Leslie, and Heather McLeod Grant. *Forces for Good: The Six Practices of High-Impact Nonprofits*. Hoboken, N.J.: Jossey-Bass, 2007.

Dawkins, Richard. *The Oxford Book of Modern Science Writing*. New York: Oxford University Press, 2009.

Drucker, Peter F. *Managing the Nonprofit Organization*. New York: Harper Paperbacks, 2006.

Editors of Writer's Digest Books. *2010 Photographer's Market*. Cincinnati, Ohio: Writer's Digest Books, 2009.

Ellis, Susan. *The Volunteer Recruitment (and Membership Development) Book*. Philadelphia, Penn.: Energize, 2004.

Emerson, Ralph Waldo. *Essays and Poems by Ralph Waldo Emerson*. Lyndhurst, N.J.: Barnes & Noble Classics, 2005.

Feinglass, Art. *The Public Relations Handbook for Nonprofits: A Comprehensive and Practical Guide*. Hoboken, N.J.: Jossey-Bass 2005.

Fennell, David A. *Ecotourism*. 3d ed. New York: Routledge, 2007.

Fitzharris, Tim. *National Audubon Society Guide to Landscape Photography*. Tonawanda, N.Y.: Firefly Books, 2007.

Flanagan, Joan. *Successful Fundraising: A Complete Handbook for Volunteers and Professionals*. New York: McGraw-Hill, 2002.

Gray-Donald, James, and David Selby. *Green Frontiers: Environmental Educators Dancing Away from Mechanism*. Rotterdam, the Netherlands: Sense Publishers, 2008.

Groopman, Jerome, and Tim Folger, eds. *The Best American Science and Nature Writing 2008*. New York: Mariner Books, 2008.

Hall, Mary, and Susan Howlett. *Getting Funded: The Complete Guide to Writing Grant Proposals*. Portland, Ore.: Continuing Education Press, 2003.

Hancock, Elise. *Ideas into Words: Mastering the Craft of Science Writing*. Baltimore, Md.: Johns Hopkins University Press, 2003.

Henderson, David. *Making News: A Straight-Shooting Guide to Media Relations*. Bloomington, Ind.: iUniverse Star, 2006.

Higham, James. *Critical Issues in Ecotourism: Understanding a Complex Tourism Phenomenon*. New York: Butterworth-Heinemann, 2007.

Honey, Martha. *Ecotourism and Sustainable Development: Who Owns Paradise?* 2d ed. Washington, D.C.: Island Press, 2008.

Humes, Edward. *Eco Barons: The New Heroes of Environmental Activism*. New York: Ecco, 2010.

Jacobson, Susan K. et al. *Conservation Education and Outreach Techniques (Techniques in Ecology and Conservation)*. New York: Oxford University Press, 2006.

Kolata, Gina. *The Best American Science Writing 2007*. New York: Harper Perennial, 2007.

Kramer, Mark, and Wendy Call, eds. *Telling True Stories: A Nonfiction Writers' Guide from the Nieman Foundation at Harvard University*. New York: Plume, 2007.

Leopold, Aldo. *A Sand County Almanac.* New York: Ballantine Books, 1990.

Leslie, Clare Walker. *Into the Field: A Guide to Locally Focused Teaching.* Nature Literacy Series, Vol. 3. Great Barrington, Mass.: Orion Society, 2005.

McBee, Shar. *To Lead is to Serve: How to Attract Volunteers & Keep Them.* West Perth, Wash.: SMB Publishing, 2002.

McIntyre, Catherine. *Writing Effective News Releases: How to Get Free Publicity for Yourself, Your Business, or Your Organization.* Colorado Springs, Colo.: Piccadilly Books Ltd, 2007.

McKibben, Bill. *The Age of Missing Information.* New York: Random House Trade Paperbacks, 2006.

Mill, Robert Christie. *Resorts: Management and Operation.* Hoboken, N.J.: Wiley, 2001.

Morello, Steven. *The Traveling Nature Photographer: A Guide for Exploring the Natural World Through Photography.* Atglen, Penn.: Schiffer Publishing, 2008.

Mowat, Farley. *Never Cry Wolf: The Amazing True Story of Life Among Arctic Wolves.* New York: Back Bay Books, 2001.

Muir, John. *The Yosemite.* New York: Modern Library, 2003.

Orr, David W. *Earth in Mind: On Education, Environment, and the Human Prospect.* Washington, D.C.: Island Press, 2004.

Owen, David. *Green Metropolis: Why Living Smaller, Living Closer, and Driving Less are the Keys to Sustainability.* New York: Riverhead Hardcover, 2009.

Patterson, Carol. *The Business of Ecotourism.* Bloomington, Ind.: Trafford Publishing, 2007.

Rouse, Andy. *Concepts of Nature: A Wildlife Photographer's Art.* Camden, London: Aurum Press, 2008.

Salzman, Jason. *Making the News: A Guide for Activists and Nonprofits.* New York: Basic Books, 2003.

Sand, Michael A. *How to Manage an Effective Nonprofit Organization: From Writing and Managing Grants to Fundraising, Board Development, and Strategic Planning.* Franklin Lakes, N.J.: Career Press, 2005.

Schwartz, Debra A. *Writing Green: Advocacy & Investigative Reporting About the Environment in the Early 21st Century.* Baltimore, Md.: Loyola College/Apprentice House, 2006.

Shaw, John. *John Shaw's Nature Photography Field Guide.* New York: Amphoto Books, 2001.

Sobel, David. *Beyond Ecophobia: Reclaiming the Heart in Nature Education.* Great Barrington, Mass.: Orion Society, 1999.

Thoreau, Henry David. *Walden.* Boston, Mass.: Beacon Press, 2004.

VandeVrede, Linda B. *Press Releases Are Not a PR Strategy.* Scottsdale, Ariz.: VandeVrede Public Relations, 2007.

Vaughn, Jacqueline. *Environmental Activism: A Reference Handbook (Contemporary World Issues).* Oxford, London: ABC-CLIO, 2003.

Weaver, David. *Sustainable Tourism.* New York: Butterworth-Heinemann, 2007.

West, Bernadette. *The Reporter's Environmental Handbook.* 3d ed. Piscataway, N.J.: Rutgers University Press, 2003.

Wilson, Marlene. *Visionary Leadership in Volunteer Programs: Insight and Inspiration from the Speeches of Marlene Wilson.* Philadelphia, Penn.: Energize, 2008.

Worsley, Dale and Bernadette Mayer. *The Art of Science Writing.* New York: Teachers & Writers, 2007.

Wyss, Robert L. *Covering the Environment: How Journalists Work the Green Beat.* Mahwah, N.J.: Lawrence Erlbaum, 2007.

Zinsser, William. *On Writing Well* (30th Anniversary Edition). New York: Harper Paperbacks, 2006.

Zuckerman, Jim. *Shooting & Selling Your Photographs: The Complete Guide to Making Money with Your Photographs.* Cincinnati, Ohio: Writers Digest Books, 2003.

Index

Entries and page numbers in **bold** indicate major treatment of a topic.

A

Action Without Borders/Idealist. org 19
Adams, Ansel vii, 103
The Age of Missing Information (McKibben) vii
American Association of Grant Professionals 82
American Association of Society Executives and The Center for Association Leadership 12, 19
American Hotel and Lodging Association 29
American Management Association 12
American Planning Association— Transportation Planning Division 136
American Public Transportation Association 137
American Society of Journalists and Authors 90, 128–129
American Society of Media Photographers Inc. 110
American Society of News Editors (ASNE) 89, 91
American Society of Travel Agents 37
Andersen, Tom 115, 117–118
ASNE (American Society of News Editors) 89, 91
Association for Research on Nonprofit Organizations and Voluntary Action 82
Association of Fundraising Professionals 74, 82–83
Association of Leaders in Volunteer Engagement 20

B

Bennett, Henry Hamilton 102
Bernays, Edward 113
bloggers 86
Boyle, Robert 122
Burroughs, John 84
Burson-Marsteller 113

C

campaign coordinators 40
Cape Cod Montessori School 47–49, 54
Carnegie, Andrew 68, 76
Carson, Rachel 39
Center for Environmental Education (CEE) 50, 54–55
Center for Responsible Travel 29
Centers for Ocean Studies Education Excellence 55
certified fund raising executive (CFRE) 71
Cervino, Kathyrn vii, 4–7, 11
CFRE International 71, 74
Clean Air Act 47
Clean Water Action 44
Coastal Preservation Network (College Point, New York) 4–7, 12
Committee for Public Information 113
communications managers/ directors. *See* publicists, green nonprofit organizations
community outreach coordinators 40
Council for the Advancement of Science Writing 129
Council of Public Relations Firms 117, 119

D
development officers. *See*
fund-raisers, green nonprofit
organizations
directors, green nonprofit
organizations 1–13
advancement 10
earnings 10–11
educational requirements 7–9
employers 9–10
employment outlook 11–12
exploring the field 9
high school requirements 7–8
history 1–2
information on 12–13
job, described 2–4, 6–7
organizations 12–13
postsecondary training 8
requirements 7–9
starting out 10
work environment 11
directors of volunteers, green
nonprofit organizations 14–20
advancement 18
earnings 18
educational requirements 16–17
employers 17
employment outlook 19
exploring the field 17
high school requirements 16
history 14–15
information on 19–20
job, described 15–16
organizations 19–20
postsecondary training 16
requirements 16–17
starting out 17–18
work environment 19

E
Earth Day 46–47
Earth Liberation Front 39
ECOCLUB.com 37
ecomanagers, green hotels/resorts
21–29
advancement 27–28
earnings 28
educational requirements 26

employers 27
employment outlook 28–29
exploring the field 26–27
high school requirements 26
history 21–22
information on 29
job, described 22–23
organizations 29
postsecondary training 26
requirements 26
starting out 27
work environment 28
eco-resorts. *See* ecomanagers, green
hotels/resorts
Ecotour Directory 35
ecotourism (defined) 30–31
ecotourism agents/planners 30–37
advancement 35–36
earnings 36
educational requirements 33–34
employers 35
employment outlook 36–37
exploring the field 34–35
high school requirements 33
history 30–31
information on 37
job, described 31–33
organizations 37
postsecondary training 33
requirements 33–34
starting out 35
work environment 36
ecotours 93, 97
EcoTours of Oregon 93, 100
Elk Lake Lodge (North Hudson,
New York) 24–25
Emerson, Ralph Waldo 84
Energize, Inc. 17–18, 20
environmental activists 38–45
advancement 43
earnings 43
educational requirements 41–42
employers 42
employment outlook 44
exploring the field 42
high school requirements 41
history 38–39
information on 44–45
job, described 40–41

organizations 44–45
postsecondary training 41–42
requirements 41–42
starting out 42–43
work environment 43–44
**environmental education program
directors 46–55**
advancement 53
earnings 53
educational requirements 50–51
employers 52
employment outlook 54
exploring the field 51–52
high school requirements 50
history 46–47
information on 54–55
job, described 47, 50
organizations 54–55
postsecondary training 50
requirements 50–51
starting out 52–53
work environment 54
environmental educators 56–66
advancement 64
earnings 64
educational requirements 61–62
employers 63
employment outlook 65
exploring the field 62–63
high school requirements 61–62
history 56–57
information on 65–66
job, described 57–61
organizations 65–66
postsecondary training 62
requirements 61–62
starting out 63
work environment 65
Environmental Protection Agency
(EPA) 46, 56–57, 66
Environmental Protection Agency—
Envirofacts Data Warehouse 45

F
Field School for Environmental
Organizing 40
The Foundation Center 12, 74, 83
Franklin, Benjamin 38–39, 68

**fund-raisers, green nonprofit
organizations 67–74**
advancement 73
earnings 73
educational requirements
70–72
employers 72
employment outlook 74
exploring the field 72
high school requirements 70–71
history 67–69
information on 74
job, described 69–70
organizations 74
postsecondary training 71
requirements 70–72
starting out 72–73
work environment 73

G
gift coordinators. *See* fund-raisers,
green nonprofit organizations
gift officers. *See* fund-raisers, green
nonprofit organizations
"The Gospel of Wealth" (Carnegie)
68
Grant Professionals Certification
Institute 79
grant proposal 76
**grant writers, green nonprofit
organizations 75–83**
advancement 80–81
earnings 81
educational requirements 78–79
employers 80
employment outlook 81–82
exploring the field 79–80
high school requirements 78
history 75–76
information on 82–83
job, described 76–78
organizations 82–83
postsecondary training 78–79
requirements 78–79
starting out 80
work environment 81
Green Corps 40–41, 45
Green Lodging News 26–27

green nonprofit organization
   directors. *See* directors, green
   nonprofit organizations
directors of volunteers. *See*
   directors of volunteers, green
   nonprofit organizations
fund-raisers. *See* fund-raisers,
   green nonprofit organizations
grant writers. *See* grant writers,
   green nonprofit organizations
publicists. *See* publicists, green
   nonprofit organizations
Greenpeace 44
green reporters 84–91
   advancement 89
   earnings 89
   educational requirements 86–88
   employers 88
   employment outlook 90
   exploring the field 88
   high school requirements 86
   history 84–85
   information on 90–91
   job, described 85–86
   organizations 90–91
   postsecondary training 87
   requirements 86–88
   starting out 88–89
   work environment 90

H
Halley, Edmund 122
Hill & Knowlton 113
Hines Tours Inc. 93
Holtcamp, Wendee 125
Hooke, Robert 122
hotels. *See* ecomanagers, green
   hotels/resorts

I
Idealist.org 9, 17, 19, 43
inbound tour guides 92–101
   advancement 98
   earnings 99
   educational requirements 95–97
   employers 98
   employment outlook 100

   exploring the field 97–98
   high school requirements 95
   history 92–93
   information on 100–101
   job, described 93–94
   organizations 100–101
   postsecondary training 95–96
   requirements 95–97
   starting out 98
   work environment 99
Independent Sector 83
Institute of Certified Professional
   Managers 13
Institute of Transportation
   Engineers 136–137
International Association of Business
   Communicators 119–120
The International Association of
   Tour Managers—North America
   98, 100
International Council on Hotel,
   Restaurant, and Institutional
   Education 29
The International Ecotourism
   Society 37

J
Jarzobski, Joanne 47–51
Jobs for Change 42
Journal des Scavans 121
journalism. *See* green reporters
J. Paul Getty Museum 110

K
Kolb, Emery and Ellsworth 102–103

L
Lee, Ivy 113
Leeuwenhoek, Anton van 121–122
Leopold, Aldo 39, 84–85
Ludlow Massacre 113

M
Maho Bay, U.S. Virgin Islands 22,
   29

McKibben, Bill vii, 40
Muir, John vii, 39, 84

N

National Association of Science
  Writers Inc. 129
National Education Association 55
National Environmental Policy Act
  (NEPA) 132
National Management Association
  13
National Marine Educators
  Association 55
Natural Resources Defense Council
  47
Nature 122
The Nature Conservancy 44, 97
nature photographers 102–111
  advancement 108
  earnings 109
  educational requirements 105–
    107
  employers 107–108
  employment outlook 109–110
  exploring the field 107
  high school requirements 105–
    106
  history 102–103
  information on 110–111
  job, described 103–105
  organizations 110–111
  postsecondary training 106
  requirements 105–107
  starting out 108
  work environment 109
Nature Photographers Network 111
Nature's Best Photography 108
NEPA (National Environmental
  Policy Act) 132
Newton, Isaac 121
New York State Forest Rangers 96
New York University 116
"The Nonprofit FAQ" (Idealist.org) 9
nonprofit organization
  directors. *See* directors, green
    nonprofit organizations
  directors of volunteers. *See*
    directors of volunteers, green
    nonprofit organizations

  fund-raisers. *See* fund-raisers,
    green nonprofit organizations
  grant writers. *See* grant writers,
    green nonprofit organizations
  publicists. *See* publicists, green
    nonprofit organizations
North American Association for
  Environmental Educators 55, 65
The North American Nature
  Photography Association 111

O

Oceana 44
outreach coordinators 40

P

philanthropy 67–69
Philosophical Transactions 121–122
photographers. *See* nature
  photographers
Pierce, Frank 68
Planeterra 35
Pruyn, Robert 21
publicists, green nonprofit
  organizations 112–120
  advancement 118
  earnings 118–119
  educational requirements 116–
    117
  employers 117
  employment outlook 119
  exploring the field 117
  high school requirements 116
  history 112–114
  information on 119–120
  job, described 114–116
  organizations 119–120
  postsecondary training 116
  requirements 116–117
  starting out 117–118
  work environment 119
Public Relations Society of America
  120

R

Rainforest Alliance 44
Regenold, Stephen 22

reporters. *See* green reporters
resorts. *See* ecomanagers, green
hotels/resorts
Rockefeller, John D. 68, 76, 113
Ruben, Adam 40

S

Santanoni Lodge 21–22
Science 122
science writers 121–129
advancement 127
earnings 127–128
educational requirements 124,
126
employers 126
employment outlook 128
exploring the field 126
high school requirements 124
history 121–122
information on 128–129
job, described 122–124
organizations 128–129
postsecondary training 124
requirements 124, 126
starting out 126–127
work environment 128
Sheridan, Mike 24–25
Shiras, George, III 103
Sierra Club 45
Sierra Nevada: The John Muir Trail
(Adams) 103
Silent Spring (Carson) 85
Society of Environmental Journalists
91
Standard Oil 68
"Starting a Career in Science
Writing" (Fazekas and Austin)
127
stock photography 104
The Sustainable Tourism
Certification Network of the
Americas 33–34
Sustain Lane 137

T

Tax Reform Act 69
Tholin, Kathryn 3
Thoreau, Henry David 84

Tocqueville, Alexis de 75–76
tour guides. *See* inbound tour
guides
transportation planners 130–137
advancement 135
earnings 135
educational requirements 133–
134
employers 134–135
employment outlook 136
exploring the field 134
high school requirements 134
history 130–131
information on 136–137
job, described 131–132
organizations 136–137
postsecondary training 134
requirements 133–134
starting out 135
work environment 136
travel. *See* ecotourism agents/
planners
Travel Industry Association of
America 101
The Travel Institute 33
Twitter.com 113

U

United States Tour Operators
Association 101
USA.gov for Nonprofits 13
U.S. Board of Education 66
U.S. Department of Education
63
U.S. Environmental Protection
Agency (EPA). *See* Environmental
Protection Agency
U.S. Green Building Council 66
U.S. Public Interest Research Group
45
U.S. Travel Association 37

V

volunteer coordinators 16
Volunteering in America 20
Volunteer Management Resource
Center 17
volunteer managers 16

Volunteer Match 43
volunteer programs. *See* directors
  of volunteers, green nonprofit
  organizations

World Federation of Science
  Journalists 129
World War I 113
World Wildlife Fund (WWF) 70

W

Ward, Charles 68
Westchester Land Trust 115
Wilderness Act 85
Wilson, Woodrow 113
World Conservation Union
  97

Y

Yarmouth, Lauren 58–61
Yosemite National Park 39
Young Men's Christian Association
  (YMCA) 68–69
YRG Sustainability Consultants
  58, 60–61, 66